BAD BOSSES RUIN LIVES

The Building Blocks for Being a Great Boss

BAD BOSSES RUIN LIVES

GREAT BOSSES ENRICH LIVES

DEBRA COREY & KEN COREY

Cover designed by Colin Goad

Edited by Chloe Thompson

Typesetting and publishing by UK Book Publishing

www.ukbookpublishing.com

ISBN: 978-1-916572-66-9

We dedicate this book to our children, Chloe and Anthony. We hope that they never have to face bad bosses, and that they grow into great bosses themselves.

CONTENTS

Preface 1

Introduction 5

Part 1 - Types of Bad Bosses 18

    Introduction 19

    The Avoider 26

    The Ignorer 33

    The Hoarder 39

    The Unappreciater 45

    The Pretender 51

    The Blocker 58

    The Firefighter 65

    The Micromanager 71

    The Blamer 78

    The Coercer 83

    Moving from Awareness to Acceptance 91

Part 2 - The Great Boss Building Blocks 94

    Introduction 95

    Empathy 103

    Compassion 112

    Authenticity 120

    Vulnerability 132

    Respect 142

Trust 153

Listening 166

Communication 178

Feedback 188

Appreciation 196

Development 207

Coaching 214

Empowerment 222

Inspiration 232

Where to begin 240

Conclusion 241

Acknowledgements 243

Appendix A 246

Appendix B 251

PREFACE

Written by Debra Corey, Co-Author of "Bad Bosses Ruin Lives" and of additional books on people and management.

This book began with a story that sparked an idea and a phrase, and that phrase has become a movement and catalyst for change...

A few years ago, as I was brainstorming with my co-author on our book *Build it: The Rebel Playbook for Employee Engagement*, I shared a story that aligned with a discussion we were having on the role and impact that bosses have. It was a very personal and emotional story, and at the end, I summed it up by saying that "bad bosses ruin lives." The phrase stuck in more ways than I imagined, even such that we put it on stickers, t-shirts, and even baby onesies.

As I traveled the world speaking at events about the book, handing out our stickers, and marveling at how people lined up to get the t-shirts, I soon discovered something very interesting. It didn't matter the country, the job level, or even the person – almost everyone had their own bad boss story, whether they had a bad boss or even if they were brave enough to admit they'd been one themselves.

Since then, I've wanted to write this book to share my stories and those of others as well as solutions, in the hopes that we can *do something* about this problem that doesn't seem to be going away. So say it with me: No one deserves to *have* a bad boss, no one deserves to *be* a bad boss, and no one deserves to *have their life ruined* by a boss! Bosses exist to *enrich* lives, not to ruin them!

MY BAD BOSS STORY

So here's the thing. Though the phrase was coined in my previous book, I realized I've never actually shared the story. Well, it's time to share it with you now…

I had my dream job. I loved the company, my role, and the people I was working with. And at the beginning, I even loved my boss. Yes, she was demanding, but I could handle that. I had been a competitive gymnast and triathlete, I could handle the pain!

That was until I couldn't anymore. When it got out of control, to put it in a nutshell, she was making my life a living hell! Nothing I did was ever good enough, and even though I was producing work that for previous bosses had been considered exceptional, this boss was challenging and slamming me for anything and everything I did.

It felt like I was stuck on a carousel of pain, which was exhausting both physically and mentally. And with the added pressures of being a one-income family at the time, I didn't know what to do but to forge on.

I vividly remember the moment when the concept of "bad bosses ruin lives" became crystal clear to me. I'd come home after another horrible day at work, where my boss had made me feel inadequate and incompetent (as usual). For months, I'd try to move past this. Come home, say a quick hello to my family, cheerfully say "I'll be right back!" and walk around the block to muster up the energy to put on my "game face" for my family. And for a time, it worked. Until that day.

About five minutes into the walk my then 11-year-old daughter came running up beside me to ask if I was okay. I decided to tell her part of the truth, admitting that I was having a hard time at work. She gently put her arm around me and easily took on the role of a parent, telling me that everything was fine. "If you're that unhappy at work, why don't you just leave?" she said. If only it was that easy!

But then ... as I listened to my sweet and sensitive daughter, I thought to myself, how did it get to this? How did I let my job ruin me, ruin my home life, and impact my family? And, what kind of mother and role model was I being to my children? And so I decided to walk away, from a job and company that I loved, and from my bad boss.

This story, and the many I've heard from others, bring my phrase to life, showing that when you have a bad boss it doesn't only ruin things for you at work, making it painful and difficult, but at home as well. And that's because **it's almost impossible to magically walk through the physical or virtual door from work to home and not have it impact how you feel and act in your personal life.**

CONFESSION: I'VE BEEN A BAD BOSS

Another reason I wanted to write this book is that besides *having* a bad boss, I, too, have been a bad boss. Why am I sharing this with you? Well, a few reasons:

First, because I believe it's important to **be honest and accept** if and when you've been a bad boss or have had bad boss traits.

Next, to show that I've **learned and grown** since accepting this, taking the actions that have helped me be a better boss. I'd like to say that I'm a great boss, but I'm too tough on myself to ever say that. If I can change, I know that anyone can.

And finally, to show that this book represents the **duality of my experiences**. Having had a bad boss and at times even being one myself, I can see and understand the problem, but also the opportunity.

MEET MY CO-AUTHOR

Speaking of duality, I felt that I shouldn't write this book alone, that it needed different experiences and perspectives to contrast and at times, challenge my thinking. Enter my co-author (and incredible husband), Ken Corey. As an Engineering Leader, he's had very different experiences to me, being the yin to my yang and offering different, but connected views. With both of our perspectives, he has helped make the book richer and more relatable.

MEET OUR CONTRIBUTORS

They say it takes a village to raise a child and let me tell you that this book truly needed our "village," which includes over 20 experts who have contributed to this book (their names appear in the Acknowledgements section at the end of the book). They are a great mix of business leaders, academics, and authors, all bringing different perspectives and advice.

And if you learn half as much as we did when interviewing them, you are well on your way to being a great boss! Thank you to all of those who contributed to this book, and thank you for joining us on this journey to be a great boss.

INTRODUCTION

The majority of bosses do not wake up in the morning and say to themselves, "Today is a great day to ruin my people's lives." And yet time after time, person after person, that is exactly what is happening, with well-intentioned bosses getting it wrong. Instead of being the great boss they want and need to be, they are doing the opposite of what they set out to do – making bad decisions, taking bad actions, and causing bad impacts.

But this isn't new, we've heard for years that bad bosses are rampant in the workplace. How people leave bosses and not companies (57%[1] of people surveyed said they left their company because of their boss). How people don't trust their bosses (64%[2] of people surveyed said that they'd trust a robot more than they'd trust their boss). And how a bad boss can drive disengagement (managers account for at least 70%[3] of the variance in employee engagement scores). We laugh at these bad bosses, point fingers at them, blame them, and even come up with nasty names to call them. But where has that gotten us? Nowhere, as we still have a very real problem! In fact, almost 100% of the people who participated in the survey we conducted for this book said that they've had a bad boss.

That's because for many of us, we don't even know that we have these traits, or we're embarrassed of them. This needs to change. If we're ever going to rid the world of bad bosses, we need to change how we look at them, how we look at ourselves, and what we do about it. We need to accept the fact that there are bad boss traits in all of us, *not just the few*. Bad boss traits are not taboo to discuss, rather we need to

---

1   DDI study, 2019.

2   Oracle and Future Workplace study, 2020.

3   Gallup, *State of the American Manager*, 2015.

understand them so that we can accept those that apply to us, *instead of denying that they exist.* And, equip ourselves with new skills so we're able to tackle our bad boss traits, *instead of trying to be a great boss using bad boss techniques and approaches.* We need to walk into them and not away from them!

By doing this, we're set up to deal with all that comes our way, good and bad, easy or hard, ready to wake up in the morning and say to ourselves, "Today is the day that I can enrich my people's lives."

WHY DO WE HAVE BAD BOSSES?

We don't set out to be a bad boss. It often creeps in quite slowly. We have a bad day, a challenging project, a difficult employee, or possibly even a bad boss ourselves. And then a sinking feeling hits you ... have you become the bad boss that you had always dreaded?

Sound familiar? I'd be surprised if it didn't. We believe it's happening because of a lack of three things – awareness, acceptance, and action – all of which we'll be tackling throughout the book.

- **Awareness** – We all have blind spots, not being aware of the big and little things that we say and do that cause us to be a bad boss.

  How we'll tackle this: In Part 1 we name them, sharing the 10 types of bad bosses, and the traits associated with them so you can understand exactly what they are.

- **Acceptance** – We're not looking in the mirror, accepting the bad boss traits we have so that we can take ownership and responsibility for them.

  How we'll tackle this: We provide tools to help you understand what your bad boss traits are, and the areas you need to focus on to change, adapt, and develop.

- **Action** – We're not taking the right actions, or leveraging the right knowledge, skills, and tools to become great and overcome our bad boss traits.

  How we'll tackle this: In Part 2 we provide you with the Great Boss Building Block™ model, containing 14 building blocks to help you develop your great boss skills.

There's a big gap in bad boss acceptance

For this book, we ran two surveys, both asking questions regarding the 10 types of bad bosses you'll learn more about in this book. One survey asked about *bosses you've had*, and one asked about *you as a boss*.

Some of the results were fairly consistent, with **99.6% of respondents saying that they've had a bad boss**, and **80% saying that they have been a bad boss**. That was a good start, admitting that bad bosses do exist, and people admitting that they may have some of these traits.

But when it comes to *what type* of bad boss people think they are, that's where it got surprising.For example, for the Unappreciater, 81% said that they've *had* this kind of bad boss, however **only 14%** said they've *been* this kind of bad boss. For the Avoider, 80% said that they've *had* this kind of bad boss, however **only 15%** said they've *been* this kind of bad boss. And for the Coercer, 72% said that they've *had* this kind of bad boss, however **only 8%** said they've *been* this kind of bad boss. This gap highlights that there's more work we all need to do to accept and then action these bad boss traits. While the theory of a bad boss exists, there's more work to be done to properly identify those types of bosses in our day-to-day to meet our employees' ever-changing needs. Luckily, this book will help you on that journey!

Myths and misconceptions

Another reason we have so many bad bosses is because of the myths and misconceptions that exist. Here are seven that we'll be busting throughout the book, highlighting them so that you and others don't repeat them yourself.

1. **All bad bosses know that they're bad bosses** – I'm absolutely sure that if we went to the bosses of those we surveyed, the majority would be shocked to hear that their employees thought they were a bad boss. But mathematically

that can't be right. We know that bad bosses exist. This is why it's even more important for you, as a boss, to be self-aware, understanding why, when, and how you may take on bad boss traits, and then overcome them to take actions to be a great one.

2. **You're either a bad, good, or great boss** – When it comes to being a boss, it is never either/or, all, or nothing. We all have a mix of traits, some bad, some good, and some great. The reality is that there are shades of gray. They come and go based on the situation, the person, and even what's happening in our lives. The key is understanding what they are, and how you can deal with and improve them.

3. **Everyone wants the same things from their boss** – If all our people were the same, life would be so easy, and being a great boss would be easy. We'd have one set of instructions to learn, and use them over and over again with our people. But that's not how it is. Your people all want and need different things from you, and for this reason, you need to understand and adapt so that we can be a great boss to each and every one of them, whatever that looks like.

4. **There are only a few skills you need to learn to be a great boss** – Just like there is not one set of instructions, there aren't one, two, or three skills to learn, and bang, you're a great boss. If only! There are a wide variety of skills you need to learn so that you can handle all that your people, your business, and the world throw at you.

5. **Once you get it right it's smooth sailing** – Wouldn't it be great if once you finished this book, or any book, or took a course, and presto, you had what it took to be a great boss? It would, but it isn't! And that's because being a great boss requires introspection and feedback, it requires commitment

and devotion, it is not simple and it is not easy. And to make it even more challenging, just when you think you've mastered something, things change, and what worked one day in one situation and with one person, may not work the next day. If you want to be a great, or at least a good boss, you need to practice, and at the same time adopt a flexible and fluid attitude and approach, setting you up to ride the waves and keep on sailing.

6. **You get promoted because you're a great boss** – Wrong, you get promoted to be a boss because you were able to do your previous job well. And though this can help you teach your people all that you've learned, it's not automatically going to make you a great boss. In fact, as a new boss, you're going to have to let go of being the person who knew everything, the person who had all the answers, and the person who focused on your performance. You'll need to do things very differently going forward. As Ryan Hawk says in his book *Welcome to Management*, "**Being a great manager has nothing to do with how well you performed in your old job.**"

7. **Bad bosses don't ruin lives** – Not every bad boss ruins lives, for as we've said, there are different degrees and levels of bad bosses. But we've heard the stories, we've had it happen to us personally, and we can say without hesitation that there are definitely bad bosses who are indeed ruining lives. They are having such a profound impact on how they're making their people feel at work that they can't walk away from it, shake it, or wash it off, and they bring it home. Home to their family, their friends, and their lives. As a boss, we know this is the last thing you want to do. That's why we are on this mission to set you up for success, being a great boss who sends your people home after a rewarding day at work to have a great day and a great life.

"The truth will set you free. But first, it will piss you off!"
— *Gloria Steinem*

The changing role of a boss

New bad bosses get created because, quite frankly, the role keeps changing, making it harder and harder for us to be a great boss. So just when you think you've figured it out, another change, challenge, or requirement comes your way! Just look around you. Your workforce is different, more diverse than ever with five generations working side by side, the workplace is different, with new work arrangements and AI impacting how and where work gets done, and expectations from our business, customers, and people are different as well. Add it all up, and being a boss is more challenging than ever!

As Josh Bersin and Janet Mertens explain in *The Definition Guide to Leadership Development: Irresistible Leadership*, "Rather than focusing on 'execution first' management tools and traditional leadership models, post-industrial leaders practice what we call 'human-centered leadership.' In the Industrial Age, we relied on management science, directed leadership, and top-down execution to thrive. In this new era, we need leaders who understand the people issues in their organizations, creating execution through inspiration, mission, purpose, collaboration, learning, and of course accountability. Instead of people being a 'means of production,' people 'are the product.' Whether you are developing software, delivering healthcare, or producing food or drugs for sale, the entire customer experience is dependent on people. Every company, in a sense, is now in the people business."

> "The time has come for business to start thinking of people as human beings and not resources; shifting from maximizing profits and profitability to focusing on how we can help people achieve their highest potential and purpose – which will naturally, positively impact results."
> — *Clare Edwards, BrainSmart People Development*

THE IMPACT AND SHADOW YOU CAST

So why does it matter? Why should we put in all of this blood, sweat, and tears into being a great boss? Is it really going to make a difference? The simple answer is yes. Throughout the book, we'll be sharing with you what happens when you get it right and when you get it wrong. From factors that impact your business such as productivity, profit, engagement, and retention, to factors that impact your people such as their wellbeing, morale, and happiness, you'll see that there's no denying it ... being a great boss can help your business and people thrive, and on the flip side, being a bad boss can damage and destroy them.

The shadow you cast

Another way of describing the impact you have on your people is as your "shadow," which as the name suggests, relates to the influence, good or bad, that you have on your people. Goldman Sachs coined the phrase "Leadership Shadow," which is made up of four things[4]:

1. **What you say** – Your written and spoken words, your non-verbal cues, and even the things you say, repeat, or emphasize.

---

4   TFCG blog, Leadership Shadow #235.

2. **How you act** – Your positive and negative behaviors and actions, role modeling to your people what you expect of them.

3. **What you prioritize** – What you value, focus on, what you spend time on, who you interact with, and your routines.

4. **How you measure** – What you decide to reward, recognize, and what you hold your team accountable for.

Shadows are often unnoticed, as you may not even realize that you're casting one. It's like when you see your child saying or doing something that reminds you of yourself. Thinking, "Do I really say that?" or "Do I really do that?" And then it hits you that yes, that's you, and they're only mimicking what they've learned by watching you. This is yet another reason for this book, to help you clearly see your shadow, your impact, and then actively cast it in the direction and way you intend to.

> **"All leaders cast a shadow. The question is whether yours is blocking the sun, or inspiring others with its silhouette to strive for more." — Brad Smith, President Marshall University, Former CEO of Intuit**

Employee engagement

We can't talk about impact without talking about employee engagement, something we'll be mentioning throughout the book. And just to be sure that you're familiar and comfortable with this term, we thought we'd define it upfront. Gallup defines engaged employees as those who are "involved in and enthusiastic about their work and workplace." In my book *Build it: The Rebel Playbook for Employee Engagement* we take this definition to the next level, defining an engaged employee as someone who:

1. **Understands and believes in the direction the organization is going** so that they feel a part of something bigger than themselves.

2. **Understands how their role affects and contributes** to the organization's purpose, mission, and objectives.

3. **Genuinely wants the organization to succeed** and feel shared success with the organization.

4. **Believes that their company, and their boss, genuinely cares** about and supports them.

Study after study has shown the positive impact that employee engagement can have with respect to several critical factors. Whether it's through improved sales, profit, customer service, or the wellbeing of your people, getting it right can be the difference between your company succeeding or failing. And as a boss, you have an important role to play when it comes to employee engagement, as great bosses create an environment and lead in a way that can drive high engagement. In fact, according to one study[5], **there is a 70% variance in employee engagement scores based on a boss.** That means that your company can do everything right, but if you as a boss don't do your part in driving engagement, then it just won't happen!

Intent versus impact

And finally, another important aspect of impact is understanding the difference between intent and impact. Put simply, **intent is what we mean to say or do**, so what we're trying to achieve. And **impact is what we actually achieve**, so how it's received. And often, the effect, the impact, does not always match the intent.

---

5   Gallup, *State of the American Manager*, 2015.

It's critical to understand this in our quest to be a great boss, as this often gets in the way. For example, just the other day in a workshop I was asked about using humor in a particular situation. My response was "It depends." If the intent is to use humor in a positive way, one that will deepen understanding and your overall relationship with this person, then you need to be aware of the potential negative impact of it as well. Will it come across as insensitive or insensitive? Will it escalate the problem? Or will your people see it as a breath of fresh air, delighted that you used humor to help in a difficult situation? The key, and something we'll talk about throughout the book, is to understand your people so that you can align intent and impact, getting it right for you and for them.

Bad boss stress disorder

One of the things we heard over and over again when interviewing people for this book was the damage that a bad boss had on them. And not just damage that lasted a day or a week, but damage that lasted months and even years. After speaking to these people, we came up with the term to describe this, calling it the "bad boss stress disorder." And like any other stress disorder, they can increase the risk of mental health problems and cardiovascular disease.

We share this not to point fingers, but to raise awareness. Awareness of the profound impact that a boss can have on their people, even the strongest of them.

HOW TO USE THIS BOOK

This book is all about you, giving you what you need to **banish your bad boss traits**, or at least get them under control, and **develop some new great boss traits**. It's intended as a safe book, one where there is no judgment, but where you know that we're alongside you, guiding and helping you on your journey. It's also flexible, available when and how you need it to be, letting you dip in and out as you face a challenge and/or a new situation. And it's honest, with us sharing with you stories of when we and others haven't gotten it right so that you can learn from these lessons. As we've said a few times already, each and every one of us has or will be a bad boss from time to time. Even as we interviewed our thought leaders, every one shared at least one story of when they were a bad boss as well.

The book is divided into two parts, for as we mentioned, we want to look at and address the two sides of being a boss - a bad one and a great one.

- **Part 1: Types of Bad Bosses** – This part focuses on the 10 types of bad bosses. In it we share some of the traps you may fall into that lead you to these actions and behaviors, the consequences of these behaviors, and then finally, a few things for you to mull over to get you ready for the next part.

- **Part 2: Great Boss Building Blocks** – This part shares our Great Boss Building Block™ model, which consists of 14 different but related building blocks that help you be a great boss. You'll see that this part is twice as long as the first part, as this book is focused on giving you the tools to be great, not belaboring or focusing on being a bad boss.

Final challenges

To set you up for success, let us encourage and challenge you to do four things as you read this book, getting the most from it and for you:

1. **Leave your ego at the door** – Acceptance and change is never going to be easy. But it will be impossible if you don't open the door to it, you don't "leave your ego at the door" as the expression goes. Be willing and open to new ideas,

ways, and challenges that we will be presenting. See them as opportunities and not as punishments for how you may have acted in the past.

2. **Lean into your greatness** – You're also going to need to lean into the change, leaning into your greatness. This means that as you go through the book you need to not only open the door to new ideas, but commit fully to them, embrace them, and give them a go. If they work, great, if they don't, lean into another idea or another until you find what works for you and your people.

3. **Embrace the journey** – If it was easy to be a great boss we'd all be one. So remind yourself that it's a journey, and embrace it. Celebrate achievements, learn from stepbacks, and accept that often it's going to be progress over perfection. You have 14 building blocks to draw from, so use them to build and rebuild as you need throughout your journey, one that hopefully you can enjoy and your people and company can benefit from.

4. **Keep the end in mind** – A great boss puts their team's interest ahead of their own, and not the other way around. They do the hard things because they're the right things to do. They look inward to see how they can do their best for their people, and outward to see how their people can be their best for themselves and their company. That's what makes a great boss.

So let me ask you, are you ready to begin your journey to be a great boss? Let's go!

PART 1 – TYPES OF BAD BOSSES

INTRODUCTION

When we think of bad bosses we conjure up images of cartoon characters with steam coming out of their ears, or holding a megaphone and screaming at their poor defenseless employees. Even in "reality," we think of those depicted in movies and television (think Michael Scott from *The Office*, Miranda Priestly from *The Devil Wears Prada*, or Mr. Burns from *The Simpsons*).

And while these stereotypical bad bosses do exist, the reality is that many other types and traits exist in the real workplace, far beyond the caricature we see in cartoons or Hollywood.

I know this because I've worked for them, worked alongside them, have heard stories about them, and yes, have even been some of them myself. And therein lies part of the problem, why there are so many bad bosses in the workplace. If you don't know what the types of bad bosses are, or where to start spotting the traits and traps that lead you to show your bad boss tendencies, how can you not be a bad boss? And what's more, how can you learn how to be a great boss?

In this section we'll be tackling this problem to create an understanding and awareness of the different types of bosses, their many traits, and what might lead people to fall into these traits inadvertently. As you read through it, it's important to keep these things in mind:

- **It's not all or nothing**, you could have some of the traits that make up a particular bad boss type and therefore you can be categorized under that bad boss type.

- **It's not either/or**, you could be more than one type of bad boss. For most of us, we have a mix of the traits of multiple types of bad (and good) bosses. They're not mutually exclusive.

- **It's not static**, with us always being the same mix of bad (and good) boss types. We frequently move from one type of boss to another as situations change at our company, with our people, and even with ourselves.

- **There can be a domino effect**, with one bad boss type or trait causing another trait to emerge.

- **Even great bosses will have bad boss traits sometimes**!

We encourage you to be open-minded and honest with yourself. Start by thinking, "Is this me?" instead of putting up your defenses and thinking, "Nah, it couldn't possibly be me." Think of it as an *opportunity*, and not a punishment. Embrace, and don't ignore these bad boss traits, for that will take you one step closer to being a great boss.

WHAT'S IN A NAME?

There are many styles and approaches to naming the different types of bad bosses. Some are what I would consider confrontational, evoking a strong reaction with names such as **Bosshole** or **Soul Drainer** to name a few. Others go for a bit of humor with names such as the **Seagull** boss, who flies in, makes a lot of noise, craps over everything, and flies off, or the **Mushroom** boss, who keeps you in the dark and buries you in busy work.

We spent a lot of time, as you can imagine, "naming" our bosses. And while there is no right or wrong way to do this, we've decided on names that are more descriptive, direct, and constructive. Remember that this book should serve as a safe and inviting place to understand *yourself* better so that you can then actively overcome any bad boss traits you may have.

That being said, this section isn't going to be easy. You won't finish it thinking to yourself what a great boss you are, and how perfect you are. At least, you shouldn't! And that's because this section focuses on **awareness** – awareness of the different types of bad bosses that exist in the workplace, of the negative impact that each can have on your people, and awareness of if/how they relate to you as a boss. And like any kind of awareness, when you look in the mirror and confront your imperfections, it's bound to be uncomfortable.

But remember, doing things that make you uncomfortable is what pushes you to new heights, and in this situation, can act as a stepping stone to help you close the door on any bad boss traits you may have. What's more, you can also open the door to new great boss traits. And yes it may seem intimidating, but it's also incredibly enlightening and rewarding, both for you and your people.

I promise you this, as I've lived it myself. Let me tell you about one of my bad boss moments:

I had been in my role as a manager for about three months when one of my employees asked if they could have a private conversation with me. They looked upset and nervous, so I stopped what I was doing, and we found a quiet place to talk. After what felt like an hour, they blurted out that the team that I was managing had formed what they called the "Debra Corey Support Group." The group met every Friday and they shared stories of how I had upset them during the week, and for some, how I had made them cry.

You can imagine the shock I felt as I heard this, as well as the deep embarrassment that I had done this to my people. Now in my defense, I had just moved from the U.S. to the U.K., and what little I knew about managing was from my American bosses who had a very different style to those managing in the U.K. But even so, how could I have not known that my management style and approach were causing such problems?

The good news is that this story had a happy ending. Fueled with an awareness of my bad boss traits, I accepted them and worked on developing management skills that were culturally acceptable and right for my people. And speaking of my people, this team became one of the strongest and most effective ones I have ever managed, and I am forever grateful for their honesty in helping me become a better boss.

"Awareness is like the sun. When it shines on things, they are transformed." — *Thich Nhat Hanh, Vietnamese Monk*

TYPES OF BAD BOSSES

It's time to introduce you to the 10 types of bad bosses that we'll be exploring in detail in this section:

1. **Avoider** – An Avoider doesn't show up for their people, ghosting them, and not giving them the time, attention, and feedback they need to do their job and feel valued.

2. **Ignorer** – An Ignorer doesn't listen to what their people say. They ignore input, ideas, and perspectives from their people, thus missing out on what they have to say, and making their people feel undervalued.

3. **Hoarder** – A Hoarder withholds and keeps information to themself, or shares it in ways that don't fully meet the needs of their people.

4. **Unappreciater** – An Unappreciater doesn't show their people recognition, gratitude, or appreciation, making them feel unvalued, invisible, and unappreciated for their actions and contributions.

5. **Pretender** – Withholds the truth and any discomfort it could cause others in an attempt to please and be nice to them, giving answers they feel are wanted, and failing to give them the honesty they need and deserve.

6. **Blocker** – A Blocker prevents or gets in the way of their people's development and career progression, blocking them from achieving their goals, mastering new skills, or contributing to the company's success.

7. **Firefighter** – A Firefighter deals with situations in a reactive and urgent manner, moving people from fire to fire with no apparent strategy, impacting their ability to plan, learn, grow, and achieve more meaningful and long-term achievements.

8. **Micromanager** – A Micromanager is overly involved in their people's work, constantly controlling and prescribing what and how work is done.

9. **Blamer** – A Blamer assigns responsibility to someone(s) for a fault or wrong, casting blame and refusing to take any accountability themselves.

10. **Coercer** – A Coercer uses power in order to bully, control, and coerce processes and outcomes, expecting strict compliance and offering their people a low degree of autonomy.

To paint a clearer picture of these types of bad bosses and create that awareness, here's what we've included for each:

- **Stories** – We all love a good story, right? We like to show and tell, bringing our concepts from the abstract to reality. So we went out to collect bad boss stories to do just this. And since the wonderful people who shared the stories didn't want it to come back and bite them in the butt, for these stories we've used the name, "Pat." For those stories that are from us, Debra and Ken, we've said "I."

- **Traps** – At the start of the book, we said that we firmly believe that most bosses don't intentionally try to be bad, so for each of the types of bad bosses we've shared some of the traps that many of us fall into that lead us to these actions and behaviors. This will help you understand and acknowledge where you are now so that moving forward you can step away from these traps.

- **Consequences** – Next, we'll share some of the issues and problems that can occur as a consequence of the bad boss traits and behaviors. We've done this as it's important to understand the impact of your bad boss traits and how you can (hopefully!) avoid them in the future.

- **Things a Great Boss Ponders** – And finally, at the end of each type of bad boss we've included a few things for you to mull over. These points are meant to help you think through and reflect on what has just been shared, and get you ready for the next section of the book, which involves taking action toward being a great boss!

REVEALING THE DATA BEHIND BAD BOSSES

And now it's time for some data, as who doesn't love data? To fuel this book, we ran two surveys, both asking questions regarding the 10 types of bad bosses. One survey asked about *bosses you've had*, and the other asked about *you as a boss*. Here are the key findings:

- **The majority of people have had a bad boss(s) – 99.6%** of participants said that they've *had a bad boss* at some point in time, so almost every person who completed the survey.

- **The majority of people admit to being a bad boss –** **80%** of participants said that they've *been a bad boss* at some point in time, so a large percentage of those who completed the survey.

- **There are many types of bad bosses in the workplace** – The data shows that each of the 10 types of bad bosses included in the survey and in this book exist in the workplace. In fact, more than half of the participants said that they've had a boss who exhibits some or all of the traits of each type of bad boss with the top five as: The Unappreciater (81%), The Micromanager (80%), The Avoider (80%), The Ignorer (78%), and The Firefighter (77%).

When we asked people to report their *own* bad boss traits, the results were different. Although again each of the 10 types of bad bosses were reported, none received more than 50% saying that they exhibit some or all of the traits, with the top five as: The Pretender (47%), The Firefighter (40%), The Micromanager (39%), The Hoarder (23%), and The Ignorer (19%).

For a free copy of the detailed survey report, please go to www.badbossesruinlives.com

THE AVOIDER

Definition: An Avoider doesn't show up for their people, ghosting them, and not giving them the time, attention, and feedback they need to do their job and feel valued.

Pat's boss gave them a project to work on, something that would take six months to complete. Week after week Pat tried to meet with their boss so that Pat could check in and run any questions by them, but one by one their boss canceled or didn't show up for the meetings, saying that they trusted Pat and didn't need to meet up.

Six months later they finally met, and Pat had the opportunity to present the completed work to their boss. And … you guessed it, the boss said that it was all wrong and that Pat needed to start all over again! You can imagine how frustrated Pat was as they not only had to begin again but ended up looking and feeling completely incompetent. So sure, their boss said they trusted Pat, but it sure didn't feel that way! Instead, the project had to be redone and Pat wasted precious hours making it "just right" for what they thought their boss would want.

The first boss we'd like to introduce you to is the **Avoider**. There are two distinct but related parts to it, both having to do with the concept of avoidance and shutting people out (think of a door, physical or virtual). The first relates to time, being a ghost to your people through **avoidance** or **lack of visibility**. And when this happens, you aren't showing up for your people, ignoring their attempts to find and reach you, and thus being unavailable to provide the support they so desperately need to be successful in their jobs. It's a key way to set your people up to fail, and no one wants to do that!

"My boss would literally walk a different route to their office so they wouldn't have to approach my cube or look me in the eye." Pat

The second relates to attention, not giving your people the attention and support they need and avoiding **giving them feedback**. Avoiders often see feedback as a punishment and not a gift. The result? Your people are left in an endless loop of trying to figure out if they should continue doing what they've been doing, change directions, or give up completely.

We're seeing this more and more as new work patterns and arrangements like hybrid, remote, and flexible working emerge. Since we often aren't working in the same location or at the same time as our people, being an Avoider can happen more easily and frequently, even if it's not intentional. If you're in any of these new working environments, this might be something that you need to learn how to overcome sooner rather than later.

THE TRAPS

Some of the most common traps that we fall into that can cause these traits and behaviors to occur are:

- I **don't have the time** to act or respond differently.

- I **don't think my people want or need me** to help and support them, they're doing just fine on their own.

- I **don't understand the value** of spending more time with my team. It's not going to help or make a difference to my people or to my company.

- I'm **fearful of what would happen** if I did spend time with my people or give them feedback. It could put me in a situation I don't feel ready to handle.

27

- I am **not confident** that I have the skills or knowledge to support my people.

THE CONSEQUENCES

When these traits and behaviors exist, here's what could happen next:

People are less effective and efficient

As a boss, you know that one of the most important things you can do for your people is to help them be effective and efficient. It's your job to set them up for success and support them to do their best work. But this will only happen if you're there for them, which means showing up with your time and attention.

Imagine training for a marathon without a watch, never knowing how fast you're going, how far you've gone, and how much time and distance you have left in the run. You'd have no way of knowing whether you're on track to meet your goal and how to pace yourself throughout the run.

Think for a moment about what happens when you meet and talk with your people. Do you suggest things that they may not have considered? Do you point out problems they may encounter and then suggest ways to get around them? Do you give them words of encouragement to help them get through a rough patch? Now think what would happen if these conversations didn't take place. Wouldn't your people be more likely to make mistakes, take more time to get things done, or get frustrated with the task at hand and completely abandon it?

That's why **if we avoid our people they end up being less effective and efficient** – focusing and prioritizing on the wrong work, not raising concerns soon enough before they become issues, and acting differently than what their job requires. Add this all together, and the result is lower levels of performance and productivity from them and for your company.

We all want feedback, even when it's negative

Sometimes we think that our people only want to hear positive feedback. However, according to one study,[6] 92% of people surveyed, so almost everyone, said they'd want to receive even negative feedback if it was delivered appropriately, as they felt it would improve their performance,

---

People may feel neglected

It's not just the performance of your people that is impacted when you are an Avoider, it also impacts how they feel. Put yourself in their shoes, how would you feel if you're stuck playing hide and seek with your boss, never being able to find them? Or if all you receive in the way of feedback from them are thumbs-up emojis. What does that even mean?! I don't know about you, but I'd feel like they didn't value, respect, or quite frankly, need me.

*Pat's boss was never there for them. As much as Pat tried, they could never get their boss' time or attention, which left them feeling like their boss didn't care about them, or their work. When they finally cornered their boss, sharing their frustration and concern, their boss told Pat that **it was actually the opposite, that they were their boss' strongest performer**, which is why the boss devoted time to those that they felt needed him more. But because Pat was convinced no one cared about them, the boss was in for a shock: Pat had already found a new job and handed in their notice the same day they confronted their boss. Too little too late!*

---

6   Jack Zenger and Joseph Folkman study on feedback, 2014.

Continuous feelings of being ignored opens the door to a big, ferocious storm from your employees. The knock-on effect of avoiding your people leads to employees who are continually stressed and burned out due to the lack of time, attention, and feedback you're giving to them. In fact, according to one survey[7], over a third (35%) of employees said their manager failed to understand the impact they had on their people's mental wellbeing, and that bosses impact their employees' mental health (69%) more than doctors (51%) or therapists (41%).

How is your response time?

With the advances in technology, one article[8] states, "**Speedy responses have become a paradigm in the workplace.**" Whether it's email, texts, or something like Slack, our people are coming to us rapid-fire through technology and, as in their personal lives, they've been conditioned and expect immediate returns. And if they don't get it, they could feel like you're avoiding them. That's why it's important that you understand what your people need, and what you can do, and set clear expectations to manage how quickly and in what way you'll respond to them.

Your people won't develop

And finally, by avoiding your people you can negatively impact their development, which is critical to them in the short and long term. Whether you believe it or not, your presence and guidance helps your employees! Consider their reactions and gratitude when you spend time with them and are focused on answering their questions, giving them feedback, and pointing them in the right direction. As a boss,

---

7   UKG's Workforce Institute, *Mental Health at Work: Managers and Money*, 2022.

8   Bryan Lufkin, *The crippling expectation of 24/7 digital availability*, 2022.

you're helping them learn and grow. Take this away, and they lose this valuable asset – you!

Spending real time with your employees helps you understand what skills and experience they need to develop and progress in their careers. What's more is that you've most likely been in their shoes yourself, and you can give them valuable insight to further enhance their development. Lastly, the ongoing feedback will set them up for development targets, which you can monitor to get them on the right track.

> **"Time is your most precious gift because you only have a set amount of it. You can make more money, but you can't make more time. When you give someone your time, you are giving them a portion of your life that you'll never get back. Your time is your life. That is why the greatest gift you can give someone is your time."**
> — *Rick Warren, author*

THINGS A GREAT BOSS PONDERS

Did you recognize any of these traps? If you think you're an Avoider boss, here are a few things to ponder to change your ways:

- ☐ What can I do to make myself available to my people? What takes up the most of my time that I could change to spend more time with my people?

- ☐ How can I open up my physical or virtual doors to my people, even if I'm not physically there with them in today's working environments?

☐ Am I giving my people the feedback they need even when I know it's going to be challenging? Am I shying away from giving feedback because it's "too difficult?"

☐ What additional skills do I need to learn to give feedback in a more open and meaningful way?

☐ If I don't deal with these situations or issues that I'm seeing from my people, what will happen? Am I headed towards a perfect storm of problem after problem?

THE IGNORER

> **Definition:** An Ignorer doesn't listen to what their people say. They ignore input, ideas, and perspectives from their people, thus missing out on what they have to say, and making their people feel undervalued.

Pat was attending their weekly team meeting, where the team would get together and brainstorm ideas and actions. It was something Pat looked forward to each week, and spent a lot of time thinking of what to present because they loved sharing ideas. But this meeting was different.

As the meeting progressed Pat got more and more frustrated, for every time they presented an idea, their boss would brush it off or give her a cursory and dismissive nod, moving their attention to another member of the team.

To make things worse, minutes later when a colleague presented an idea almost identical to Pat's, their boss made a big deal about it, congratulating them on their great suggestion. And though the colleague tried to give Pat credit after the fact, it didn't help them feel anything other than neglected and disrespected for their idea being ignored in the first place.

The next type of boss moves from avoiding to ignoring, **ignoring our people by not listening to them**. It should come as no surprise that listening to your people is essential, helping them feel valued and heard, coupled with a sense of belonging. Listening, along with taking their feedback seriously, can be the difference between being a high-performing team that consistently attracts and retains top talent and a disengaged team that falls behind its competitors.

But too often, us bosses don't put in the effort to listen to our people as they try to share with us their unique and valuable thoughts and perspectives. When this happens it makes me think of the Charlie Brown comic where his teacher is talking and all you see and hear is "Wah wah woh wah wah." No one is listening and no one is interested. We never really know what that teacher could have offered to her students because no one ever took the time to give her a voice!

"Leaders who don't listen will eventually be surrounded by people who have nothing to say." — *Andy Stanley*

THE TRAPS

Some of the most common traps that we fall into that can cause these traits and behaviors to occur are:

- I **don't have the time** to take in information differently. Why do I need to adapt my own style?

- I **don't think my people want or need** to share information with me.

- I **don't need** the thoughts and perspectives of my people. What will they add that I don't already know?

- I feel like I lack the **skills, knowledge, and/or confidence** to take in information.

THE CONSEQUENCES

As a consequence of these traits and behaviors, some or all of these problems can occur:

Your people won't feel heard

There's a famous quote from Dr. Martin Luther King's 1967 speech at Stanford University where he said "Riots are the voice of the unheard." To put it in context, it came at a time following two separate race riots, and this was his opportunity to try to explain the cause of rioting to a predominantly white audience. This quote and his speech were not condoning riots but were meant to call out that if we ignore rightful demands (e.g. the voice of people), some will inevitably take the issue into their own hands.

This feeling of not being heard is just as important in the workplace. Sure, they probably would not riot, but they could respond by not showing up physically or emotionally. This inevitably impacts their ability to perform and achieve their objectives. What's more, they could just leave you entirely. In fact, according to one study[9], 41% said that they left their job because they didn't feel listened to.

> According to global research[10] by The Workforce Institute, 83% of employees think they aren't listened to "fairly or equally" at work. But it gets worse, as almost half (47%) say that underrepresented voices aren't being heard, and over half (60%) believe their views and opinions are ignored.

A knock-on effect from this is that your people feel excluded and may even feel ostracized. In Cong Liu and Jie Ma's book, *Workplace Ostracism*, they explain how ostracism in the workplace occurs when employees are excluded, dismissed, sidelined, or ignored. They go on to share the negative effects this can have on the company as well as their employees, leading to anger, depression, anxiety, and emotional exhaustion among those who experience it.

---

9   All Voices, *State of Employee Feedback* study, 2021.

10   The Workforce Institute, *The Heard and the Heard-Nots* report, 2021.

Your people will shut down completely

Have you ever been in a meeting when your boss ignored or shot down your ideas or challenges? Few things are as embarrassing or demoralizing – you end that meeting feeling like no one is listening to you, and that you're "talking to a brick wall," as the expression goes. So why bother speaking up at all?

This feeling is exactly what happens when you don't listen to their people. And because of this, after a while they shut down, saying to themselves – why try if no one is going to listen to me? Why put in the time and effort to speak up if it's not going to be taken seriously? The seemingly simple act of ignoring and not listening to your people closes the door on their contributions, insights, and innovation, as well as their minds, hearts, and souls.

Ideas (and problems) are missed

Innovation is another factor that is critical to businesses, impacting whether yours ultimately succeeds or fails. You only need to compare Blockbuster and Netflix, two companies that started out doing the same thing, but with only one surviving solely down to innovation. And because of this, your company needs every one of your people contributing to innovation, not just you. And if you're not listening to them, then you're going to miss each and every one of these unique ideas.

Great ideas can come from anywhere (and anyone)

One of my favorite examples of a great idea came from one of our employees at a LEGOLAND theme park. His job was to let people onto rides, and day after day he saw firsthand the frustration parents faced trying to entertain their energetic and excited children standing in line, waiting to get on the ride.

His idea was to set up tables in the middle of the lines containing LEGO blocks. Here, children could safely play while their parents stood in line and watched them having a great time. Brilliant idea, and something that could only have been suggested by someone who was close to the problem, and heard by a boss who was listening.

Watch out for that iceberg

It's not just the great ideas that are missed when you don't listen to your people, it's the problems as well. And as we all know about problems, if we don't address them they can end up much worse than how they began. My favorite model for explaining why we need everyone out there identifying and calling out problems is Sidney Yoshida's "Iceberg of Ignorance," which he developed back in 1989. It highlights that the majority of problems are hidden from bosses (96% at the very top of his model), and if we don't do anything about it we'll hit "icebergs." I don't know about you, but I'd rather have these problems spotted and resolved than risk sinking the "ship!"

Iceberg of Ignorance

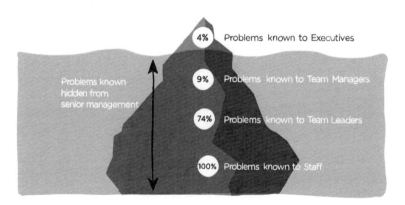

4% Problems known to Executives

Problems known hidden from senior management

9% Problems known to Team Managers

74% Problems known to Team Leaders

100% Problems known to Staff

THINGS A GREAT BOSS PONDERS

Did you recognize any of these traps? If you think you're an Ignorer boss, here are a few things to ponder to change your ways:

☐ What can I do to encourage my people to speak up, and how can I create a safe space for them to share their thoughts, opinions, and concerns?

☐ How can I adapt to not always being physically with my people? Can I find different ways to let their voices be heard?

☐ What am I doing to give myself the time and space to listen to my people? Am I being fully and actively engaged with what they have to say?

☐ What additional skills do I need to learn in order to improve my ability to listen to my people in an active and meaningful way?

☐ Am I considering what will happen if I don't listen to my people? What will I miss out on? What will they miss out on?

THE HOARDER

> **Definition:** A Hoarder withholds and keeps information to themself, or shares it in ways that don't fully meet the needs of their people.

Pat's team was always going through reorganizations, with their boss always trying to find that "perfect" way to be structured so they'd work in the most effective and productive way. Each time they were told it was the last one, and each time the changes that were made had a huge impact on almost every member of the team.

So when Pat's boss let it slip that they'd be going through another round of reorganizations, you can imagine the fear and doubt it caused within the team. They asked their boss for more details but were told that they'd have to wait a few weeks as they weren't ready to share it with them. The result was that Pat and the team felt like they were frozen in time, not knowing what to do and how to act as they awaited their fate. Without understanding what they were up against, the feelings of mistrust grew between the boss and the team, and a few of them even left the company, stating that this was the final straw for them.

The next boss on our list is a Hoarder. When you think of a hoarder, you immediately picture someone surrounded by an excessive, and often nonsensical, number of items. **But when it comes to bad bosses, it's less about items and more about information.**

And these days, in such a fast-moving world, one where so many of us are no longer sitting side-by-side in an office, information is even more important than ever. It's what keeps us connected, in the know, and armed with what we need to do our best work and stay on top of what's happening in our companies and with our colleagues. And as a boss, it's your responsibility to share this information with your people in a meaningful and effective way so that they have what they need when they need it.

But too often this doesn't happen, with bosses **hoarding information by withholding and keeping it to themselves**, and actively not sharing it with members of their team who desperately want and need it. Or, they may share information, but in a way that ignores and/or doesn't address and meet the needs of their people, like in the case of Pat's Avoider boss.

> **"If you want people to make the same decisions that you would make, but in a more scalable way, you have to give them the same information you have."**
> — *Keith Rabois, American technology executive and investor*

THE TRAPS

Some of the most common traps that we fall into that can cause these traits and behaviors to occur are:

- I **don't have the time** to share information with my people.

- I **don't think my people want or need** me to share information with them.

- I assume my people **already have the information** from a different source or channel

- Since I'm **unclear and uncertain** as to what I'm actually allowed to share, sharing nothing is the safer option.

- I lack the **skills, knowledge, and/or confidence** to share the information in the best way.

THE CONSEQUENCES

As a consequence of these traits and behaviors, some or all of these problems can occur:

Business-as-usual comes to a crawl

In the business world, speed is critical. It can be the difference between a company succeeding and failing. As bosses we need to do everything we can to enable speed, removing barriers and hurdles so that our people (and business) have a clear path to the "finish line."

But if you hoard information, you negatively impact this all-important speed. It slows you down because your people will need to come to you to obtain or clarify information, which sucks up your valuable time. What's more, it will slow your people down, too, as without the proper information, they will run into continuous hurdles that they don't understand how to overcome. Had they received the right information in the first place, they could have done their jobs faster and worked smarter, not harder.

In a world where many of our people are working remotely and workforces are often global, it's even more important to ensure the flow of information happens swiftly and effectively.

Poor communication = poor company performance

Research[11] by the Economist Intelligence Unit shows how poor communication can have a tremendous impact on the workplace, undermining the performance of employees and their company. The most significant impacts of this poor communication were found to be:

- **Stress** – 52% said it caused them more stress.

- **Performance** – 44% said it caused a delay or failure to complete a project.

- **Morale** – 31% said it negatively impacted their morale.

- **Performance** – 25% said it caused them to miss their performance goals.

- **Innovation** – 20% said it created obstacles to innovation.

Efficiency is derailed

Let's say you get away with being slower, that your business isn't bothered when it takes slightly longer as long as you get over the "finish line." Can you say the same when it comes to being less effective and efficient? Will your business accept mediocre results, ones that don't meet the needs of your clients, customers, and shareholders?

If you hoard information, you impact the effectiveness of your people as you're setting your people up to be less efficient. And, importantly, this is not their fault! Because they don't have the information they need to do their job, they can make mistakes (because they're forced to make assumptions, which often are the wrong ones), do unnecessary work (because they're not getting the direction they need), and/or get frustrated, demotivated and disengaged (which can impact their overall performance).

---

11   The Economist Intelligence Unit, *Communication barriers in the modern workplace*, 2018.

> ### Miscommunication leads to mistakes
>
> Over 60% of errors in the workplace can be traced back to a failure in communication. By changing how you communicate with your people, it can reduce the number of errors, and thus mistakes, that are made. Remember, your people and your business will benefit from fewer errors and mistakes.

Negatively impacts how your people feel

If you were running a race, let's say it's a marathon, and throughout the race, you receive no information, nothing telling you where you are and how much longer you have to finish the race. How would this make you feel? If it was me, I'd feel frustrated and demotivated, almost to the point of giving up.

As a hoarder, your inactions directly impact how your people feel. And why not? Put yourself in their shoes, with a boss who is withholding information, or sharing it in a way that doesn't help your day-to-day. You'd feel frustrated, right? Wouldn't you feel like you weren't trusted? Wouldn't you feel disengaged and demotivated? Now you're getting it: The answer to all of these questions is a resounding **yes**!

"Employees who suspect that their boss is withholding valuable information experience the slow leaking of their spirits, confidence, and dedication to your company's success. That's because they don't feel like their success is your number one priority. A boss who shares information is intent upon helping each person step into the best version of their personal self every day." — *Garry Ridge, Chairman Emeritus WD-40 Company & The Culture Coach*

THINGS A GREAT BOSS PONDERS

Did you recognize any of these traps? If you think you're a Hoarder boss, here are a few things to ponder to change your ways:

- ☐ Am I sharing information with my people as part of my regular interactions with them? Am I making sure they have what they need when they need it?

- ☐ How can I better understand how the information I receive will affect my people? Am I asking myself if this is something they need and deserve to know?

- ☐ When I share information with my people, what am I doing to put myself in their shoes? Am I taking steps to understand things from their perspective so that my communication lands with them?

- ☐ What additional skills do I need to learn in order to communicate in a meaningful and effective way?

- ☐ What will happen if I withhold information and/or don't share the full story with my people? Have I thought about the potential mistakes and problems that could occur if I don't share this information?

THE UNAPPRECIATER

> **Definition:** An Unappreciater doesn't show their people recognition or gratitude, making them feel unvalued, invisible, and unappreciated for their actions and contributions.

When Pat saw a problem in one of the company's key systems, they volunteered to take charge and own it. It was in a dire state when Pat first began, but thanks to their efforts the problems were fixed, and the system was soon up and running. As their boss announced this huge achievement at a department meeting, Pat stood by waiting for the boss to mention their name, to congratulate Pat for all that they had done. But instead, their boss took the credit and did not even mention Pat's name or their contributions.

And to add fuel to the fire, at the next all-company meeting their boss was publicly recognized for this work, and when asked to tell everyone about it, still did not bother to show appreciation to Pat. You can bet that this was the last time Pat would volunteer to help out their boss, let them sink or swim themselves!

While the last type of bad boss focused on hoarding information, this type focuses on hoarding something different, appreciation. And while you may think that appreciation isn't as important as information, let me tell you that it absolutely is. Appreciation can help connect us with our people, inform them so they can perform at their best, and show them that you value and – yes, you got it – *appreciate* them.

If you hold back appreciation, you're missing out on these powerful moments to capture and celebrate the good and great work and contributions that your people are making.

You're leaving them scratching their heads and wondering if what they've done is right, is good enough, or seen in the first place. And for this reason, delivering what I call the "appreciation feeling" has been proven to drive awareness, productivity, profit, wellbeing, and a myriad of other positive results for your people and your business.

"People will forget what you said. People will forget what you did. But people will never forget how you made them feel." — *Maya Angelou, author and poet*

THE TRAPS

Some of the most common traps that we fall into that can cause these traits and behaviors to occur are:

- I **don't have the time** to show appreciation.

- I **don't think appreciation is important** to my people, they don't want or need it.

- My people **already feel appreciated** when receiving their paychecks, bonuses, etc, so there is no need for anything more.

- I **don't know when or how** it's appropriate to give appreciation.

- I **don't have extra funds** to deliver monetary rewards, so why bother?

> **Recognition does not need to cost a lot of money**
>
> According to one study[12], 72% of employees said that a simple "thank you" would make them feel more motivated and help build morale. This shows that you don't need to spend a lot of money to make your people feel appreciated.

THE CONSEQUENCES

As a consequence of these traits and behaviors, some or all of these problems can occur:

People are less effective and efficient

When we spoke about the Avoider boss, we shared the problems created when feedback is not given and how it can make your people less effective and efficient. And since appreciation is a form of (positive) feedback, the same thing can happen when it is withheld.

Take the results of a study[13] that looked at 41 fundraisers responsible for soliciting alumni donations to a university. In this study, a director visited half of the fundraisers in person, telling them, "I am very grateful for your hard work. We sincerely appreciate your contributions to the university." The second group received no such expressions of gratitude. The results found that the expression of gratitude, the appreciation given, increased the number of calls by more than 50% for the week, while fundraisers who received no thanks made about the same number of calls as the previous week.

---

12   Reward Gateway, Global Recognition Report, 2017.
13   Francesca Gino and Adam M. Grant, Journal of Personality and Social Psychology, 2010.

"Receiving expressions of gratitude (appreciation) makes us feel a heightened sense of self-worth, and that in turn triggers other helpful behaviors toward both the person we are helping and other people, too." — *Francesca Gino, Harvard Business School professor and best-selling author*

Other studies have found similar results, with one[14] reporting that 79% of employees said they'd work harder if their efforts were appreciated, and another[15] reporting that 82% of employees said that praise and recognition are leading factors in helping them improve their job performance. However you slice or report it, the data shows the tangible difference appreciation can make to a company. So when it's not given, the impact can be far-reaching and significant to the overall performance of your people and company.

Negatively impacts wellbeing at work

When people feel appreciated it can impact how they feel, which is why, as said in the previous point, it can impact how they perform. One effect is that they are happier and more motivated thanks to what science calls the "dopamine effect," which is when you get a hit of the "feel good" neurochemical dopamine when you are appreciated, which by the way, is the same chemical released when you eat chocolate, but no calories. And when you deprive your people of appreciation, it deprives them of this chemical release and of this wonderful feeling.

But it doesn't stop there, for the impact of appreciation goes far deeper than simply making employees feel good. A simple "thank you" or

---

14   Reward Gateway, Global Recognition Report, 2017

15   Gallup, *Employee Recognition: Low Cost, High Impact,* 2016.

"well done" not only has the power to lift the mood of your people, but it can support your employees' overall wellbeing, something that we're all interested in and something that needs to be addressed by showing appreciation.

One way is by lowering levels of stress, which can have a profound impact on the wellbeing of your people. This is thanks to another neurochemical, the stress hormone called cortisol. One study[16] found that there was a 23% reduction in cortisol after appreciation was given, thus suggesting that an "attitude of gratitude" can lower your levels of stress, making you more resilient and able to handle the stressors and challenges that employees often face.

Appreciation can also help prevent or reduce burnout, something that is increasingly on the rise due to symptoms of the more fast-paced, complex, and demanding modern workplace. It does this by addressing some of the factors that can lead to burnout such as feelings of unfair treatment at work, unclear communication from managers, and lack of manager support. Supporting this, one study[17] found that when appreciation is done effectively, 73% of employees are less likely to always or very often feel burned out.

Pat and their team were told that they had won team of the year, which was a prestigious award at their company. The award was based on a large piece of work the team had worked really hard on, doing so while their boss was out of the office. Pat couldn't believe it when their boss took full credit for the work and even demanded that the award sit on their desk. So much for letting Pat and the team receive the appreciation they deserved!

---

16   McCraty R, Barrios-Choplin B, Rozman D, Atkinson M, Watkins AD, *The impact of a new emotional self-management program on stress, emotions, heart rate variability, DHEA and cortisol*, 1998.

17   Gallup/Work Human, *Transforming Workplaces through Recognition*, 2022.

Your company may see increased turnover

The final problem has to do with retention. We often believe that pay is the number one reason people leave a company, but in fact, a study[18] found that a whopping eight out of 10 employees (79%) who quit their job cited a lack of recognition and appreciation as the key driver. And for those who have not left their company, another study[19] found that employees who do not feel adequately recognized and appreciated are twice as likely to say they'll quit in the next year.

To put this in context, assuming you have a team of 10 people and show none of them appreciation, at the end of the year you will only have one person left. Can you afford to lose almost your entire team?

THINGS A GREAT BOSS PONDERS

Did you recognize any of these traps? If you think you're an Unappreciater boss, here are a few things to ponder to change your ways:

- ☐ What am I doing to make sure that I don't miss the great things my people are doing? Am I on the lookout for great work so that I can then show them appreciation for what they've achieved and done?

- ☐ What can I do to make appreciation a more natural habit in my day-to-day routine?

- ☐ What additional skills do I need to learn in order to show my people appreciation in a meaningful way?

- ☐ How will my people feel and what will they do if I withhold appreciation from them?

---

18   Reward Gateway, Global Recognition Report, 2017

19   Gallup, *Employee Recognition: Low Cost, High Impact*, 2016.

THE PRETENDER

Definition: A Pretender withholds the truth and any discomfort it could cause others in an attempt to please and be nice to them, giving answers they feel are wanted, and failing to give them the honesty they need and deserve.

Every time that Pat's boss went to the monthly department head meeting the team would hold their breath. What would their boss agree to this time? How much extra work and pain would it cause them? Their boss was such a yes-man, never pushing back and telling the truth, being more concerned about how it would look if they said no, completely ignoring the effect it had on their team. This meant that time and time again Pat and the team had to work overtime, work weekends, whatever it took to get the work done and deliver on their boss's habit of overpromising deliverables.

The straw that broke the camel's back, and finally convinced Pat to hand in their resignation, was when their boss agreed to complete a project in the middle of the holiday season in five days knowing darn well that it would take them 10 days. So while everyone around them was attending holiday festivities both in the office and at home, Pat and the team were stuck in the office. Stuck working because their boss didn't have the backbone to just say no!

When we described the last type of bad boss, the Unappreciater, we explained that by not giving their people appreciation they were in essence not giving their people chocolate by withholding appreciation. This next type of boss, the Pretender, is so desperate to be liked that they put on a mask for their team and for their own bosses so no one knows there's an issue, and offer too much "sweetness" in the form of sugarcoating every little thing.

What motivates and drives us to act in this way is twofold. The first has to do with **wanting everyone to like you** and doing everything you can to achieve this outcome. This includes pretending that everything your people are doing is fine, and not sharing with them any negative feedback or truths that could potentially upset or cause them not to like you. The second has to do with **wanting everyone to be happy**, to be calm, and to pretend that everything is fine so you don't cause waves or ripples. This includes hiding the truth from your people and not giving them "tough love" for fear of upsetting them.

And of course, being liked and keeping your people happy is important, but we need to remind ourselves that this is not the primary focus of our job. By pretending that everything is OK and avoiding conflicts or discomfort, this boss is withholding information that could help their people do their jobs even better or be happier and more productive at work. So it's time to take off the mask and make sure you're being open and honest with your people.

> "A boss's job is not to win popularity contests. A boss's job is to point out to people as clearly and with as many specifics as possible when they are doing a bad job, AND when they are really doing a good job." — *Kim Scott, CEO of Candor, author of Radical Candor and Just Work*

THE TRAPS

Some of the most common traps that we fall into that can cause these traits and behaviors to occur are:

- I **don't have the time** to deal with and handle the difficult stuff.

- I **don't think my people want or need** me to share information or feedback with them.

- It's better to **only deal with positives** and not negatives because there's no benefit in dealing with an overly difficult situation.

- **I want to protect my people's feelings** so I don't want to share any negative or difficult information with them.

- I like to **be seen** as a positive and optimistic boss and don't want to bring my team down with the negatives.

- I lack the **skills, knowledge, and/or confidence** to handle these situations.

THE CONSEQUENCES

As a consequence of these traits and behaviors, some or all of these problems can occur:

People are less effective and efficient

I won't lie, I love eating sweets. However, eating too many of them can cause negative health effects such as weight gain, blood sugar problems, and an increased risk of heart disease. And for this reason, I limit how many I eat (okay, I try). The same is true when it comes to having too many false truth "sweets," which impact the health and performance of your people, making them less effective and efficient, impacting the health of your company.

To illustrate this, let me share a story from Kim Scott's book titled *Radical Candor*:

Bob joined Kim's team with glowing references, an amazing career at two of the world's greatest technology companies, and a quirky, charming personality. There was just one problem: Bob's work was terrible. After a few weeks of working diligently, he finally made a presentation that was essentially a "jargon salad." His slides were riddled with sloppy mistakes – whole sections were cut and pasted, and he hadn't even bothered to make the fonts consistent.

Kim didn't say a word to him after he showed it to her because she was so mad she was afraid she might say something "mean." So she procrastinated. For 10 months. It got so bad that his poor work had cost the company months, and that now they would have to raise more money, diluting everyone's stock and bringing them one big step closer to failure. And to make it even worse, several of her best employees said they'd quit if Kim didn't fire Bob.

This story highlights the significant impact that not giving honest feedback can have on performance, perpetuating bad performance in our people. When you put caring too much above hurting the feelings of your people, you, as Scott calls it, are exhibiting "ruinous empathy." And like anything ruinous, it can cause disasters in how your people act and what they can and cannot achieve.

More mistakes are made

Mistakes happen, we all know this, but as a boss, it's our job to do what we can to prevent them from happening, and deal with them when they do occur. But when we're a Pretender this doesn't happen, we are in essence inviting and welcoming mistakes into our organization. Just think of the example shared above, where Bob made mistake after mistake, was never told, and was never held accountable. And for this reason, Bob's mistakes kept freely and continuously flowing into the organization, impacting Bob, his team, and the entire company.

And it's not just our people's mistakes that happen when we're a Pretender, but our own as well. And that's because we're so focused on the positive, the sunshine, that we don't want to admit or share when there is a bit of rain or darkness, which includes when we make a mistake. So we pretend that it hasn't happened, sweep it under the carpet, and hope that the mistake doesn't cause too many problems. And because a boss typically will be a role model for their team, it's more likely that your people will see you doing this and they'll wind up doing the same thing themselves, creating even *more* mistakes along the way!

Stalls learning moments

I always joke and say that I learn more from when things go wrong than from when things go right. In fact, each book I write (including this one), is filled with examples of mistakes I've made and lessons I've learned. And for this reason, when you withhold giving your people the cold hard truth, feedback on mistakes that they've made, you are robbing them of their development. That's why I'm a big fan of calling mistakes "learning moments," as that's exactly what they are.

These learning moments help your people have a clear understanding of how they can adapt their working habits and avoid mistakes. Without this they will continue making the same mistakes over and over again, hindering their personal growth and development. To illustrate this let me go back to my days of doing gymnastics, where making a mistake was actually painful (picture falling off or on a four-inch balance beam, ouch!). If my coach wasn't constantly pointing out when I was doing something wrong, and suggesting new ways to perform a skill, I never would have overcome the challenges and developed new ways to successfully (and safely) achieve it.

It can be exhausting

Last, but not least, are the problems that being a Pretender can cause to you, the boss. And that's because quite frankly it can be tiring to continually wear a mask and pretend that everything is great. Because inevitably we experience things that are disappointing, discouraging, or frustrating. And when life throws us lemons, we can't always make lemonade! Your team needs to understand that, and that means showing the good *and* the bad.

When thinking positive actually makes you feel worse

A study[20] was done that surveyed undergraduate students to find out how negative thoughts and emotions might play out in their lives. Students were asked to respond to questions like "I tell myself I shouldn't be feeling the way that I'm feeling" (where 1=never or very rarely true and 5=very often or always true).

The research found that people who are more accepting of their negative thoughts and emotions had greater wellbeing and satisfaction with life, with fewer symptoms of depression and anxiety as well.

You need to remind yourself that it is not your job to please everyone, to only deliver good news, and to make sure that everyone is happy. You're not helping yourself, exhausting yourself on this positivity treadmill, and you're not helping your people. By the way, I learned this lesson the hard way when I had a boss who told me that I acted like a cheerleader, always being positive, and upbeat, and never coming to him with bad news. Lesson learned, pom poms put away!

---

20   Brett Q Ford, Phoebe Lam, Oliver P John, Iris B Mauss, PsycINFO Database Record, 2018,

THINGS A GREAT BOSS PONDERS

Did you recognize any of these traps? If you think you're a Pretender boss, here are a few things to ponder to change your ways:

☐ Am I being honest and truthful with my people? How can I start from a place of truth instead of automatically holding back information that might be difficult to share?

☐ How can I meet difficult situations head-on instead of avoiding them and letting them get out of control?

☐ Would it be better for my people to get the truth from me, instead of someone else?

☐ What additional skills, e.g. improved communication or messaging, learning how to deliver feedback, do I need to learn so that I feel more comfortable sharing negative information with my people?

☐ Don't my people deserve and need to hear the truth? Is it really as bad news as I think it is?

THE BLOCKER

> **Definition:** A Blocker prevents or gets in the way of their people's development and career progression, blocking them from achieving their goals, mastering new skills, or contributing to the company's success.

Pat had been at their company for five years. They had watched colleague after colleague get promoted to be a manager, while Pat's feet were firmly stuck in their current job. So much so that it felt that they were super glued there, even though Pat was recognized time and time again for the great work they were doing. When they asked their boss what it would take to get promoted, Pat was given empty assurances and runaround responses such as "Take a few more courses to learn some new skills," "You need more visibility within the business," or even "Mentor someone else on the team." Even as Pat tried to do all these things, they were constantly passed on when it came time for promotions.

When they'd had enough, Pat decided to talk to their boss's boss and hear what they had to say about Pat's opportunity to be promoted. Pat was surprised when the senior boss said that Pat's boss had told them that Pat didn't want to be promoted, that they were happy in their job and wanted to stay there working for their current boss. Nothing like being there for me boss, thought Pat! Soon after, Pat quit their job and went on to be a manager at their biggest competitor.

In American football, there is a position called a blocker. Their sole purpose is to obstruct or hinder players from the other team, preventing them from tackling the quarterback and ending the play. And in sports, this makes sense as your objective is to win by stopping your opponent from scoring. But when it comes to people management, you should never see yourself as getting in the way of others!

Unfortunately, that is exactly what a Blocker boss does, blocking **and preventing their people from progressing in their careers**. Going back to the Pat story, it was their boss that got in their way. For although Pat had done everything their boss had asked of Pat, and was even receiving recognition for their efforts, Pat was constantly losing in the promotion game. It could have been for legitimate reasons in that Pat wasn't ready to be promoted, or it could have been because their boss was merely getting in Pat's way. Either reason, it resulted in Pat feeling blocked and demotivated for not being able to move forward.

Next, a Blocker can **obstruct the visibility and voice of their people**, not standing up for and being an advocate for them. This is important not only when it comes to career progression, but also as a good manager to be an advocate for them and wave the proverbial flag to show your support.

And finally, a Blocker **can get in the way of change**, being resistant, opposed to, or unwilling to do things differently. While this might not be a *person* that the Blocker is up against, you are still getting in the way of change, innovation, and improvements, thus blocking future company success. As Daniel Tuitt said, "The ability to forget old ways of doing things is as important as learning new things."

THE TRAPS

Some of the most common traps that we fall into that can cause these traits and behaviors to occur are:

- I don't think my **people want or need** me to support them in this way.

- My **business is doing just fine** with the tried-and-true ways of working, and won't benefit from making any changes.

- I **don't think it's a priority** for my people to figure out how to fuel growth through development and innovation.

- I **don't know what will happen to me** if my people progress in their careers or succeed "too much."

- I **don't know how** to be an advocate for my people, or I don't think I need to be.

THE CONSEQUENCES

As a consequence of these traits and behaviors, some or all of these problems can occur:

People's skills will fall behind

The success (or failure) of your company is highly dependent on the performance of your people. And as you also know, the key to performance is development, with your people learning and mastering new skills that will help them be more effective and efficient. But what you may not know, or may not have seen at your company, is that the pace of change in the workplace has never been higher. In fact, one report[21] found that 85% of the jobs that will exist in 2030 haven't even been invented yet, meaning the majority of your people will need to learn and develop new skills in order to perform the jobs your company requires for the future. Crazy to think about, but it's true. And, as the report says, "The ability to gain new knowledge will be more valuable than the knowledge itself."

---

21   Dell Technologies and the Institute for the Future, 2017.

If we block this development, we directly impact the performance of our people. One study[22] found that nine out of 10 employees (90%) agreed or strongly agreed that training and development programs improved their job performance. By supporting and encouraging your people's development, you're enabling your people to be more effective and efficient. At the same time, your people will be able to navigate their work more effortlessly, resolve issues quickly, and see things with a more experienced perspective. That's a win for you as a boss, for them as an employee, and for your business which will benefit from a more skilled workforce!

People lose a sense of purpose at work

Developing your people not only impacts their performance, but how they feel about their company and themselves. Providing the means to support their development shows that you care about them – and, importantly, that you believe in them. Learning, developing, and progressing in your career path can create positive feelings of accomplishment and achievement, which can boost self-confidence and self-esteem, and build a sense of purpose and connection with others. Add this all together, and by blocking your people's development and career progression the health and wellbeing of both your company and people are negatively impacted.

Pat was working with their manager on a project to analyze a situation in the company, finding new and innovative ways to solve it. They worked together to prepare a presentation that they were going to both present to the CEO. One day Pat came into work to find out that their boss had decided to go ahead and present their work to the CEO without Pat, and to make things worse, had taken Pat's name off of the presentation. No surprise, Pat was both frustrated and pissed off, saying "I can only guess, but I'm pretty sure that my CEO didn't even know that I had done most of the work."

22   The International Journal of Business and Management Research, 2019.

Stifles creativity and innovation

As mentioned previously, being a Blocker sometimes involves blocking new ideas and new ways of thinking being presented by your people. Instead, you rely on your own experiences and ideas, using the same steps and past assumptions over and over again without trying to discover new insights and approaches. Even if your own experience and ideas are good, this still creates an environment that blocks any sort of creativity, innovation, and progress.

This is something I did when I first became a boss, and not to point fingers, but I can blame it on *my* boss. And that's because when I first started the job and told him how I was planning on pulling my team together to brainstorm new ideas, he quickly put a stop to this, saying, "That's what I pay you to do!" So for years, I shied away from this, blocking and missing out on all of the wonderful insights and perspectives my team had to share, and the collaborative processes that facilitated creativity and innovation.

The importance of novice ideas

"Think back to a time when you were new or inexperienced at something. This may be a stage in your life when you attempted something challenging, important, or difficult but you were clueless and naive. To succeed you had to go outside of your comfort zone to build your understanding of this new area. At this point, you are persistent and willing to go the extra mile and this inspires innovation as you are crossing new ground. As your thirst for knowledge breeds confidence you reach out to new people through collaborating and test new boundaries through trying new things.

When looking at things as a novice means you're more open to bring in different insights to come to unique conclusions or novel ideas."

From Daniel Tuitt's article, "When Knowing Too Much Can Block Innovation"

More people leave your company

And finally, if we block the development and career advancement of our people they will decide that they're not getting what they want and need and are much more likely to leave your company. In fact, according to one study[23], a lack of development and career advancement are among the top three reasons why people leave their job.

This is more important than ever, as development and career advancement are something that younger generations entering the workplace care deeply about. This was something that was talked about when Millennials entered the workplace, and with the focus now on Gen Z, is being talked about as well. According to the LinkedIn report, employees see "opportunities to learn and grow" as the top driver of work culture, thus impacting their decision to join and stay with a company. In the report, the majority of Gen Z respondents expressed a desire for more opportunities to move up or increase responsibilities (61%) and more opportunities to learn or practice new skills (76%). They were also more likely than any other generation to agree with the statement, "I used to think learning was not worthwhile, but now I think it is." As the report says, "This shift in perception indicates adaptability and agility – two qualities that should be nurtured in a workforce."

THINGS A GREAT BOSS PONDERS

Did you recognize any of these traps? If you think you're a Blocker boss, here are a few things to ponder to change your ways:

☐ How can I best support my people's development, understanding what they really need and then playing my part in helping them achieve it?

---

23   McKinsey & Company, *The Great Renegotiation* report, 2021.

☐ What can I do to be more open-minded to the thoughts and ideas that my people present, even if change makes me uncomfortable?

☐ How much do I encourage my people to try something new, even if it doesn't always work out?

☐ What would happen if my people never developed or progressed, how would this negatively impact them? How would this reflect on my company?

THE FIREFIGHTER

> **Definition:** A Firefighter deals with situations in a reactive and urgent manner, moving people from fire to fire with no apparent strategy, impacting their ability to plan, learn, grow, and achieve more meaningful and long-term achievements.

I once had a boss who was a Firefighter, and although this was his only bad boss trait, when he acted in this way it really impacted my ability to perform at my best. That's because when my boss was wearing his firefighter "helmet" he would have us move and jump from one idea and project to another. And while there were parts of this that we felt were exciting, as it kept things fresh and new, it was also challenging as I never really understood what and why we were doing something. It also felt like I wasn't accomplishing anything, that I was leaving things unfinished before jumping into the next fire.

And speaking of jumping, one thing we sometimes did as we knew our boss would move us from fire to fire, was to ignore the request until our boss came back to us a second time. Not great, but as we'd been burned so many times (no pun intended) jumping into a fire, only to find out that we really hadn't needed to spend any time on it at all. This became our coping mechanism in dealing with this bad boss trait and instead of taking issues seriously, we would roll our eyes and think, "Here we go again!"

A Firefighter's role is to deal with emergencies, quickly and swiftly handling challenging, and at times, life-threatening situations. We rightly view them as heroes, applauding them as they extinguish flames, save people from danger, and, yes, even rescue cats in trees.

However, in the workplace, this act of firefighting can actually cause damage, especially when a boss is initiating and driving this kind of culture. Although at times the quick resolution of fires (problems) is a good thing, more often it distracts your attention from the bigger and more strategic issues and challenges that your business faces. Your focus and attention end up being misplaced, putting in place patches and plasters that won't last instead of spending time identifying and addressing root causes that can drive lasting change. And just like a fire, these underlying problems can fester, spread, and cause devastation and destruction to your business, and at the same time to your people, who are stuck in an exhausting cycle of fighting one fire after another.

THE TRAPS

Some of the most common traps that we fall into that can cause these traits and behaviors to occur are:

- I **don't have the time to** strategize and prioritize problems and work, so I try to deal with the most critical and pressing matters.

- I think **my people enjoy** moving quickly from task to task

- I believe that this is the **best way to work** to ensure that the most important and critical work gets done.

- My **working environment is very fast-paced**, and this is just how we have to do it because there's no other option.

- I **like the adrenaline rush** of doing things this way. It feels good and makes me feel important.

- I lack the **skills, knowledge, and/or confidence** to work in a more proactive, strategic, and long-term way.

THE CONSEQUENCES

As a consequence of these traits and behaviors, some or all of these problems can occur:

People (may) work harder, but not smarter

Firefighters receive extensive training to prepare them for every scenario they could potentially encounter in their jobs, and once in the fire, receive clear instructions so they can perform in an effective and efficient way. Unfortunately in firefighting situations in the workplace, this doesn't happen. More often, our people are thrown into situations with little explanation, lacking the clarity and focus they need to get through the "smoke" to achieve their objectives. Because each situation may be different, they'll likely lack the skills and experience required to handle each emergency. And even if they do succeed, the lack of direction and repetitive training means that they are in constant reaction mode, and not learning or retaining information along the way.

Firefighting also leaves your people more reliant on you, with them having to run in and out of the problem at hand to get new instructions, slowing them down and putting the work and their colleagues at risk. And finally, although a Firefighter wouldn't leave before putting the fire out or rescuing the cat in the tree, this doesn't always happen in the workplace. With a Firefighter boss moving so quickly from fire to fire, the chances of a fire being *fully* put out, meaning that the cause of the fire has been identified and can't happen again, is very rare.

The negative impact of interruptions

A study[24] was done where researchers followed around workers and timed their activities, especially every time they changed what they were working on. They found that each time workers were distracted, on average **it took 23 minutes and 15 seconds to regain focus and get back into the flow** of their original task and work.

The study also found that people compensate for interruptions by working faster. However, this comes at a price, with people experiencing more stress, higher frustration, and time pressure.

Mistakes are made

No surprise, when you're rushing from fire to fire, mistakes are made as there just isn't enough time to do things properly. This forces you and your team to find incomplete solutions, where often you put on a patch as you rush out of one fire into another, never dealing with and addressing the underlying cause.

The day before a big product was to be launched, Pat's boss decided that the team should focus on a new promotion idea to boost awareness. The boss made everyone drop what their responsibilities were to work on this new idea, even though part of the team was responsible for training the front-line staff who were going to be selling the product. As a result, on the day of the product launch, the staff felt ill-prepared to talk about the product and the team missed their sales quota.

---

24   Gloria Mark, Daniela Gudith and Ulrich Klocke, *The cost of interrupted work: more speed and stress*, 2008.

Lessons aren't learned

One of the ways that we all learn and develop is by taking the time to debrief on our work. Unfortunately, in firefighting mode, this isn't something that happens, as the constant pull of fires leaves no room to debrief and identify learnings or improve collaboration. As a result, your people will miss out on key learning moments, never having the opportunity to pause and reflect individually and collectively on what's worked and not worked.

This almost happened when I worked on an important project to bring onboard employees of a newly acquired company in just six weeks. It was a legitimate fire as it had to happen quickly, but unfortunately, since it was the first time we'd been through an acquisition, our boss gave us very little direction. The result was that try as we did, we made some mistakes, but luckily none of them were irreconcilable. The good news is that although my boss was a Firefighter in this situation, she did in the end bring us all together for a debrief so that we could learn, and at the same time develop processes and timelines so that next time we'd have to go into this kind of work we'd have the skills and processes to handle it well.

There's more risk for burnout and mistrust

As mentioned in an earlier story, sometimes firefighting can deliver feelings of excitement, with an adrenaline rush filling our bodies as we run into the fire to save the day. But at what cost? For when the adrenaline wears off, your people will feel physically and mentally exhausted, left trying to recover before they're thrown into the next fire. They won't be able to cope with this in the long term, as it's not sustainable for your people and your business.

This constant mode of firefighting can also reduce your team's trust in you because your team doesn't see or understand the direction or purpose of what they're doing. They may question if their boss is making the right decision to benefit the team, or even the business.

A culture of firefighting can also lead to greater stress at work because of its unpredictability. Not knowing if and when they'll be thrown into a fire, if they'll have the skills to deal with it, and if they'll be able to put the fire out, can cause undue stress on your people. And, no pun intended, it's way more likely that your people will burn out from all the firefighting they're forced to do!

THINGS A GREAT BOSS PONDERS

Did you recognize any of these traps? If you think you're a Firefighter boss, here are a few things to ponder to change your ways:

- ☐ How can I put more processes and priority-setting in place so that my team doesn't have to consider every fire (issue at work) a crisis?

- ☐ What can I do to re-prioritize and/or challenge others when my team is asked to jump into a fire so that I'm not setting them up to fail?

- ☐ What am I doing to ensure that we're focusing on work that has the greatest impact on the business? Does the work we're doing support and align with my team's goals and objectives?

- ☐ Do I need more support or development in project management or problem-solving so I can be a better guide for my team?

THE MICROMANAGER

> **Definition:** A Micromanager is overly involved in their people's work, constantly controlling and prescribing what and how work is done.

One day, Pat's 16-year-old intern popped into their office and broke down crying. Through the tears, they blurted out, "It doesn't matter what we do, it will never be good enough for you." These words really upset Pat, describing it as a "medicine ball hitting me in the gut." Quickly recovering, Pat pulled the team together to hear what others thought, and as they shared, the floodgates opened!

They confessed that they called Pat the "Memo Master" as they controlled the team's every action with a memo explaining exactly what they needed to do. In fact, each week they had a competition on how many memos Pat would be sending out. They also shared their frustration over Pat feeling that they needed to be around for every aspect of their job at the hotel. From being there at handovers to when they cashed out the bar and restaurant, they didn't feel that Pat trusted them as Pat was micromanaging their every move.

You'd think that having a boss who wants to be deeply involved in what you do would be great, right? How wonderful would it be to have someone who takes the time to give you direction and instructions, review and give critique to all of your work, and be there alongside you at each and every turn. That's exactly what many bosses, especially new ones, think, believing that they're doing it for their people.

However, this is far from the truth, as nothing can be more demotivating and exhausting than having a boss who is a micromanager. In fact, micromanagement is one of the most often cited characteristics of a bad boss, with eight of 10 of our survey respondents saying they've had a micromanager boss! And yes, a micromanager is there for their people, but at what cost? For instead of giving them the time, space, and autonomy to perform, their excessive control and involvement often squashes the joy and meaning out of their people's work, leaving them resentful, resistant, and frustrated.

THE TRAPS

Some of the most common traps that we fall into that can cause these traits and behaviors to occur are:

- I know that **things will get done faster** if I manage in this way, and I don't have the time to teach my people.

- I believe my **people want and need** me to manage them in this way, that it's best for them.

- Managing this way is the only way to really **help and support** my people, and to stay closely connected to them.

- I **like being in control**, and if I'm not then work won't get done and mistakes will be made.

- I **don't fully trust** my people to do their job correctly, so by managing them in this way I can make sure they're doing things the "right" way.

- I lack the **skills, knowledge and/or confidence** to delegate work and support my people working in an autonomous way.

THE CONSEQUENCES

As a consequence of these traits and behaviors, some or all of these problems can occur:

People slow down

One of the most harmful effects of micromanagement is that it can slow your people down, thus decreasing their individual and collective productivity. This makes perfect sense. Think about it, if you're continually scrutinizing and providing excessive input and control, giving them little to no autonomy, the productivity of your people will naturally decrease as this slows down processes and creates bottlenecks (you!). Studies[25] have also found that when employees are constantly being watched over they **perform at lower levels because they fear choking under pressure**.

A related side effect is that your people will become dependent on you, limiting their ability to think and act independently and take initiative, again slowing down the flow of work. For even if they believe they can handle something on their own, they'll feel the need to come to you based on assumed expectations, adding hurdles that will add unnecessary time and complexities.

Leads to lower morale

Micromanaging your people can also negatively impact how they feel in a variety of ways. The first has to do with their morale, with a

---

25   DeCaro, M. S., Thomas, R. D., Albert, N. B., & Beilock, S. L., Journal of Experimental Psychology, *Choking under pressure: Multiple routes to skill failure*, 2011.

survey[26] finding that almost **seven out of 10 (68%) of employees who said that they had been micromanaged said that it had a negative impact on their morale**. Again, this isn't surprising, is it? If you're constantly telling your people what they can and can't do, and robbing them of the opportunity to think and act independently, they will likely feel that you don't trust them. These actions will leave them feeling demotivated and unappreciated, with low morale.

So for your company, as well as your team, you'll see lower productivity but also lower employee satisfaction, and likely higher employee turnover. Why? Well, nobody wants to stay in a place where they're not trusted, don't have autonomy, and don't feel valued!

Negative toll on wellbeing

Micromanaging can also negatively impact the wellbeing of your people, particularly because of the stress that it can cause. Think of how you'd feel if you constantly had someone directing you, looking over your shoulder, questioning and challenging you at every turn. Wouldn't it stress you out? Wouldn't you constantly be worrying about what would happen next? And while it is hard to directly link micromanagement to stress and health problems, given the HSE (Health and Safety Executive) definition of stress as "the adverse reaction people have to excessive pressures or other types of demand placed on them," micromanaging is certainly a contributing factor.

Related to this, micromanaging can also lead to burnout on both sides because it is, quite frankly, exhausting. It's exhausting for your people as they feel they're constantly under the microscope, constantly being watched and checked. And it's also exhausting for you, as it's extra work and effort to be on guard at all times, and you end up being stretched too thin.

---

26   AccountTemps, Survey on Micromanagers, 2014.

Blocks employee development

When we micromanage our people, we often get in the way of or limit their opportunities to learn and grow. When we're overly prescriptive with our people we're getting in the way of their hands-on learning and experimenting. It's like tying our children's shoelaces over and over again for them instead of letting them learn how to do it themselves through trial and error. And by doing this, they never learn how to do it themself, or it takes longer to learn this task.

"If you give a man a fish, you feed him for a day. If you teach a man to fish, you feed him for a lifetime."
— *Chinese proverb*

If we micromanage our people, we don't let them learn from their mistakes, giving them the freedom to fail. And as we know, failure is absolutely critical in the learning process, as we all need the opportunities and space to make mistakes, turning them into learning moments so that we can move forward without repeating them.

Pat was famous for their red pen, using it over and over again on their people's work as a way to highlight and correct the mistakes they had made. Pat genuinely felt they were helping their team, that by pointing out what they had done wrong it would help them learn what was right. But unfortunately, it had the opposite effect, for instead of learning, seeing the red marks as a teaching moment, they were left "seeing red" as the expression goes, angered and frustrated by Pat's actions, and at the same time, damaging the team's self-esteem.

Stifles creativity and innovation

And finally, micromanaging can also have a negative impact on innovation, which is critical to business success. The reason this happens is because when you micromanage you are essentially crushing your employees' creative spirit. They think to themselves, "Why present and put any ideas forward if my boss only cares about their own ideas?"

And even if your people are brave enough to present an idea, it will most likely align with or be similar to those of their boss, since micromanaging creates a "mini-me" mentality, one where people are encouraged to think and act like their boss. And when this happens, creativity and innovation are stifled, with the richness and diversity of thought being left on the table.

It's hard for a Micromanager to understand this, but it's true: Just because your people aren't doing it your way, doesn't mean that they're doing it the wrong way.

THINGS A GREAT BOSS PONDERS

Did you recognize any of these traps? If you think you're a Micromanager boss, here are a few things to ponder to change your ways:

- ☐ What is it that's making me feel the need to micromanage? Is it a lack of trust, my own confidence, or the wrong people in jobs? Is there any way I can move away from micromanaging in this way?

- ☐ How can I give my people more freedom and autonomy? If I'm scared about it being more work, how can I free up the time to do so, knowing it will ultimately make things easier and better for me and my people?

☐ When I speak and meet with my people, what can I do to be open to and involve them in solving problems and coming up with ideas, coaching them along the way?

☐ What additional skills do I need to learn so that I give my people more autonomy and support them in a less controlling way?

☐ What impact does micromanaging have on my people, and what effect will it have on them in the short and long term?

THE BLAMER

> **Definition:** A Blamer assigns responsibility to someone(s) for a fault or wrong, casting blame and refusing to take any accountability themselves.

Let's start this section with a story from Ken...

Once I asked someone on my team to design and deliver a new technology in an area that I wasn't very familiar with. I thought they were strong and had lots of experience in this area, and because of this, would be able to do and handle most of the work. But since this person wasn't very happy and was not very engaged, they didn't do a great job, taking longer to finish it and doing so in a way that was not the most effective. And since I didn't know any better, I blindly submitted the work to my boss.

When my boss saw it, they chewed me out, telling me how bad it was. I reacted by blaming my employee, pointing the finger at them and basically throwing them under the bus, doing so hoping to not look bad to my boss. However, it actually ended up biting me in the butt for it made me look far worse, with my reputation taking a hit, and contributing to me being asked to leave the company when they ended up doing a reorganization a few months later. It was a painful lesson, but a lesson learned!

The next kind of bad boss is a Blamer, and can be defined as someone who assigns responsibility for a fault or wrong. **They believe that blame needs to be cast and that someone needs to be held accountable.** At times, this is so they can avoid criticism or keep a good reputation. We often refer to these bosses as the "Teflon Boss," because in blaming others when things go wrong or when commitments are not met, nothing sticks to them and they wind up coming out looking great.

A Blamer doesn't always need to make it about them, but they likely feel the need to cast blame in general. Regardless of the intent, blaming can lead to a variety of unhelpful and harmful emotions, such as resentment, anger, and defensiveness. And unfortunately, this culture of blame is on the rise. You only need to watch reality TV shows to see this, e.g. contestants pointing fingers at one another on *The Apprentice*, making blame seem humorous, acceptable, and almost necessary. However, playing the "blame game" never works. In fact, various studies have shown that **people who blame someone else for their mistakes lose status, learn less, and perform worse** relative to those who own up to their mistakes. Also, companies that have a culture of blame have been found to have a serious disadvantage when it comes to creativity, learning, and innovation.

THE TRAPS

Some of the most common traps that we fall into that can cause these traits and behaviors to occur are:

- I think **it's easier to blame** someone than to sort out the details of what went wrong.

- I think I'm **removing the ambiguity** by assigning blame, which helps us all move on.

- If I don't assign blame, **I worry it will cause confusion or problems** down the road.

- I lack the **skills, knowledge, and/or confidence** to handle it in any other way.

THE CONSEQUENCES

As a consequence of these traits and behaviors, some or all of these problems can occur:

People slow down

My bad boss story, the one that drove me to write this book, involved a boss who was a Blamer (among other things). We used to joke that there was a blame rota, with our boss rotating from week to week who would be blamed for any of the problems or mistakes that occurred. And although this sounds amusing, I can tell you that it wasn't!

The effect this had on us when it was our turn (and even when it wasn't) was that we were constantly looking over our shoulder, wondering when we'd be blamed for something that may or may not be our fault. Because of these insecurities, instead of doing something only once, we were doing things twice or three times, making sure that nothing would be out of order and doing things to cover our butt so there couldn't possibly be any blame assigned. And in the fast-paced world we all work in, this is something that we need to avoid, creating a safe space where our people aren't slowed down for fear of being blamed.

Curbs creativity and innovation

Another problem driven by fear of being blamed is that it halts creativity and innovation. I mean who wants to put an idea forward that in the future may come back to bite you in the butt, being blamed if it doesn't work out or causes problems? For that reason we sit quietly in the background, holding back our ideas, not contributing ones that could make an impact and difference to our teams and our company.

> **Our brain interprets blame as a physical attack**
>
> When we're blamed, our prefrontal cortices shuts down and directs all our energy to defending ourselves. Which, ironically, sabotages our ability to solve the problem for which we are being blamed.

Mistakes are hidden

This fear can also kill accountability, leading to our people hiding their mistakes. Why would your people tell you that they've made a mistake if you're only going to blame them for causing it? So instead, our people sweep their mistakes under the carpet and act like nothing has happened. The result can be catastrophic, with mistakes percolating, waiting to derail, and causing destruction to you and your company.

We need to remind ourselves that everyone makes mistakes and that it's part of being human. As a boss, it's our job to not pounce on these mistakes by casting blame. Instead, we need to minimize the damage by focusing on solutions so that the mistakes don't happen again.

Shatters morale

Finally, and no surprise considering all of the previous points, is that being blamed for something can have a significant impact on how we feel. And that's because it is such a negative experience, one that we do everything we can to avoid and forget. And according to a study[27] that measured employees' moods at work, **a negative event can affect our mood five times as much as a positive event.**

---

27   Andrew G. Miner, Theresa M. Glomb, Charles Hulin, The British Psychological Society, 2005.

"No matter how nice you think you are, every unkind word or angry tone that escapes your lips *undoes* five times the amount of good your kind words and actions may have done." — *Michael Timms, "Blame Culture Is Toxic. Here's How to Stop It"*

Because it's not just how your people feel in the moment, this negative experience can impact how they think and act in the future. Because we feel the sting of how it felt to be blamed more powerfully, we remember these moments more vividly, and our memories retain them longer.

THINGS A GREAT BOSS PONDERS

Did you recognize any of these traps? If you think you're a Blamer boss, here are a few things to ponder to change your ways:

- If things don't go to plan, how can I look at the situation from a constructive point of view, instead of assigning blame?

- What can I do to understand the underlying reasons for blaming others, e.g. fear, guilt, etc., so that I can address them?

- What additional skills do I need to learn so that I don't feel the need to blame others? Do I need to be more confident in accepting failure or mistakes?

- Am I understanding how my people feel when I blame them? Am I noticing that they are less motivated or productive?

THE COERCER

> **Definition:** A Coercer uses power in order to bully, control, and coerce processes and outcomes, expecting strict compliance and offering their people a low degree of autonomy.

Pat's boss asked them to work on a project, telling Pat that they welcomed Pat's ideas on how best to design and deliver it. They worked diligently on it, putting in two solid months of overtime to get it done. When Pat shared it with their boss, they quickly ripped it apart, changing pretty much every aspect of it.

Pat felt absolutely heartbroken. Pat had not only put their heart and soul into this project, missing out on things in their personal life by working overtime, but Pat had given their boss what they had asked for. Unfortunately what Pat learned the hard way was that although their boss said they wanted Pat's ideas, it was just an act, a facade, a pointless exercise for their boss to be seen as collaborating with their people, but in the end getting their way.

Last, but certainly not least, is the Coercer boss. We've left it for the end for a few reasons. First, because it's often the one spoken about the most, and so our concern was that if we started with it, you may not give the others the attention they deserve. Second, because many of the traits mentioned in the previous bad boss types exist in a Coercer as well, so it made sense to wait until the end, after we've covered them.

So what is a Coercer boss? The best way to describe it is through the use of one word: **Power.** And while power is not always bad, as sometimes your people need you to exert it to help them learn, grow, and get work done, like anything else, it's how you use it that can make a significant difference.

To some extent, each of the prior types of bad bosses use power, e.g. the Hoarder to hoard information, the Blocker to block development, the Micromanager to control work, and the Blamer to cast blame. But when it comes to the Coercer, they do it in *different ways*, taking it to the extreme by controlling, discounting, and disregarding the needs and wishes of their people. The Coercer will use their power in *multiple ways*, often combining the traits of a variety of different bad bosses. And, they use this power for *different reasons and motivations*, using it in a more manipulative manner to not only get things done their way but for their best interests. It's a terrible environment to be in!

> **"Fear is a normal human emotion, and – when held in check – can sometimes be a functional or even necessary way to ensure that people do not become complacent. But when fear becomes an entrenched marker of an organization's culture, it can have toxic effects over the long run." — *Andrew Carton, Wharton Management professor***

And because of this, a full-blown Coercer boss creates a reign of fear and terror by demanding and at times bullying their people. They use their power to instruct and control their people in what, when, and how to do their work, expecting strict compliance and demanding results. They use their power to be dismissive, not letting their people speak or contribute ideas, conveying that they don't value their opinions or are not interested in hearing from them. And they use their power to be manipulative, putting their needs over those of their people by not sharing information, changing goals, and ignoring the needs of their people.

As with the other types of bad bosses, there are different levels of a Coercer. For example, I can remember being at a meeting once where I was frustrated that my team just wouldn't come to a decision, standing up and telling them that we were going to do it my way because I was the boss. Was I a bully? Well, sort of because unlike Nike's slogan "Just do it," that is not a management technique. Did I ruin lives? Probably not, especially since after I said it everyone laughed (including me) as it was so out of character for me. But I was definitely being a Coercer as my reaction served no purpose, and was certainly a lesson for me going forward.

But a full-blown Coercer, one that exhibits all or most of the traits I've described, can certainly cause problems and they can certainly ruin lives. To illustrate this, here are just three of the many comments I received when asking people to share their bad boss stories:

"I often compared it to being in an abusive relationship because you never knew which version of my boss you were going to get. They were constantly playing members of the team off against one another and demanded total, unswerving, blind loyalty, however undeserved it might be."

"I would find myself double booking meetings to avoid them. My confidence was broken to the extent that I would not have faith in my own views or opinions so would not share them in any situation including my private life. I would arrive at work looking for their car in the car park and purposely find an alternative place to work."

"They made me doubt everything about myself. I felt isolated, sad, frustrated, and angry."

It is important to note that a Coercer **is not always that screaming, yelling bully** that we often think of. Going back to Pat's story, their Coercer boss was actually quite soft-spoken, never yelling at them or causing a scene. The problem with this was that Pat never saw it coming as their boss would lob grenades at them, having no time to run for cover. As Pat explained, "**My boss was a schemer, not a screamer**," but a Coercer nonetheless!

THE TRAPS

Some of the most common traps that we fall into that cause these traits and behaviors to occur are:

- I think **things will get done faster** if I just tell my people exactly what and how things need to be done.

- I think my **people want and need** me to exert this level of control over them, that it's best for them.

- I assume that this is the **best way to manage** my people and that it gets the best results for them and the company.

- I **fear that work won't get done** and mistakes will be made if I'm not constantly in control.

- I **don't fully trust** my people to do their job correctly, so by leading in an authoritarian way I make sure that my people are doing things the "right" way.

- I **don't know how** to manage in any other way, I've never been taught otherwise.

THE CONSEQUENCES

As a consequence of these traits and behaviors, some or all of these problems can occur. *Please note that the list is quite extensive, for as mentioned previously, to some extent a Coercer takes on the traits of many of the previous types of bad bosses. So although we've listed these problems, we've kept them quite brief as they've been covered elsewhere.*

Reduces efficiency

As you may recall, the Blamer boss left their people looking over their shoulders to avoid being blamed for something, which left them working slower and less effectively and efficiently. The same is true with a Coercer, where a culture of blame and fear leaves your people not only looking over their shoulder but holding their breath, waiting for the wrath that may come their way in a variety of forms of backlash.

Fear can actually hinder our cognitive abilities. When we're scared, we can't think clearly and we leave logic and reason at the door, and productivity on the table.

You become a bottleneck

Being a Coercer can slow your people down. It's not just the looking over their shoulders or being frozen and paralyzed through fear, but the dependency they'll have on you. And as mentioned for the Micromanager, this limits their ability to think and act independently and take initiative, slowing down the flow and pace of work.

People shut down

For the Ignorer, we listed the problem of people shutting down, with this happening because they felt like no one was listening to them, and that they were talking to a brick wall. The same is true with a Coercer, for in addition to this, the culture of fear they create stops their people from contributing and inputting their insights, perspectives, and innovation.

Prevents creativity and innovation

Next, a Coercer can stifle and hinder creativity and innovation, something necessary in today's competitive world. Similar to other types of bad bosses, this happens because your people feel that no one is listening to them, and that no one cares to hear their views, so they shut down and keep their ideas to themselves. They feel they are unable or not encouraged to act on their own initiative, losing their sense of accountability and ownership.

The culture of fear created by a Coercer can have two more impacts on their people when it comes to innovation. First, it can lead their people to suffer a form of cognitive paralysis, losing their ability to be imaginative and innovative. And second, it can stop people from contributing and inputting their insights and perspectives because the risks and consequences just aren't worth it to them.

> **"For people to be happy at their jobs, they desire the freedom to express creative ideas and choose their own processes. People want to feel like they're part of something bigger than themselves – rather than simply working for a paycheck." — Allaya Cooks-Campbell, learning experience designer**

Reduces employee development

For quite a few other types of bad bosses, we mentioned how they have a negative impact on their people's development, not giving their people the support and/or room to learn and grow. A Coercer does the same, and because of their need for power, they often will get in the way of their people's development because they see it as a threat to their own power.

I can relate to this, as early on in my career I had a boss who told me that as a manager I needed to know more than the people on my team, and this was why he had put me into the role. Since then I've learned how insane this was, that it's better to have a team of strong and experienced people than relying on one sole boss to know it all. Putting it another way as Methodist minister H.E. Luccock said, "No one can whistle a symphony. It takes a whole orchestra to play it."

Mental health spirals

And finally, a Coercer can have a significant impact on how their people feel. Findings have shown that when coercive power is exerted by a boss, it can create feelings of powerlessness and stress, and can often lead to anxiety, depression, low self-esteem, burnout, and mental health issues to name a few.

"Their management style was 'break them to make them' (a direct quote) and damn did my boss break me." Pat

As we've mentioned, a Coercer has many of the traits of the other types of bad bosses, which on their own causes a whole host of problems. Add one or more of these together, and it's like a boulder rolling down a hill, gathering speed and energy, having a greater impact on those at the bottom, or in this case, on your people.

And it's not just the short-term impact of this boss, but the long-term and lasting impact that they can have. I experienced this after I had the bad boss mentioned at the start of the book, where even after I'd left them I had the "scars" that had to heal. My next boss had to keep reminding me that she was nothing like this boss, that I could relax and be myself, and not worry about how she would treat me. This was something I heard time and time again when people shared their stories of having worked for a Coercer, with some sadly saying how they needed to take significant time off after they left them, had to get counseling, and even change professions because of the damage they caused.

I share this to show the profound impact that a full-blown Coercer can have through the use of power and fear both to your people and your organization. And for this reason, as Dr. Robert Sutton says in his book *Good Boss, Bad Boss*, **"You can't be a great boss if you don't keep your inner jerk in check. The damage to your followers' humanity renders you incompetent. And even if you don't give a hoot about 'warm, fuzzy people' stuff, the impaired performance ought to get your attention."**

THINGS A GREAT BOSS PONDERS

Did you recognize any of these traps? If you think you're a Coercer boss, here are a few things to ponder to change your ways:

- ☐ What is it that's making me feel the need to hold onto power so tightly, e.g. lack of trust, my own confidence, the wrong people in jobs, etc., and what can I do to let go of it?

- ☐ Do I use my power to motivate and rally my team around a cause or problem, or do I use it to step over or around my people to get things done?

- ☐ What can I do to let go of the controls I have in place, sharing the power and giving my people more freedom to thrive?

- ☐ What can I do to give my people's ideas and suggestions a chance? Why do I always need it to be "my way"?

- ☐ What additional skills do I need to learn so that I give my people more power, control, and autonomy? How can I build stronger and more effective relationships with them?

MOVING FROM AWARENESS TO ACCEPTANCE

As we end this section, there is one more thing to do, and that is to move from **awareness** to **acceptance**. So far we've been sharing lots of information on each of the types and traits of the bad bosses, which is great for awareness, but it's only the beginning of your journey.

The next phase is acceptance, where you recognize and embrace the traits that you personally need to focus on to be the great boss I'm sure you want and need to be. This is absolutely critical to get you ready for the next section of the book, which focuses on action, providing you with direction and focus.

A challenge I used to have as a young manager in dealing with stressful situations was that when I was faced with too much stress, it translated into me being impatient and sometimes sharp with my employees. Equating this to the 10 types of bad bosses, I exhibited traits of an Ignorer, Blocker and Coercer.

Accepting this, I spoke to my team to make them aware and warn them that these traits would appear from time to time, saying that it was something I was working on improving. Luckily my wonderful team laughed and joked about it, deciding that the best way to deal with it was to name this part of my personality "Debby," and give me a sign to hang on my office door in these situations that said, "Debby is in - enter at your own risk!" It was far from perfect, but it was our way of accepting and embracing my bad boss traits as I worked on overcoming them, and at the same time protecting everyone from Debby!

ASSESSMENT TIME

To help you move from awareness to acceptance, we've created an online assessment tool that you can use. By answering the questions included in it, you will gain an awareness of which bad boss types and traits you may have so that you can then do something about them.

Identifying your bad boss type(s)

If you'd like to use the free assessment tool, you can find it at: www.badbossesruinlives.com

---

If you want to skip the online tool, you can do a self-assessment by going back through the different types of bosses in this part of the book, and scoring yourself based on this scoring system:

- **1** – I have **no** traits for this type of bad boss

- **2** – I have **some** traits for this type of bad boss

- **3** – I have **many** of the traits of this type of bad boss

As you do this, it's important to be honest with yourself, remembering that we all have some bad boss traits, so accept them and think of it as an opportunity, and not a punishment. Embrace, and don't ignore these bad boss traits, for that will take you one step closer to being a great boss.

You can jot down the results in the table below:

Avoider		Blocker	
Ignorer		Firefighter	
Hoarder		Micromanager	
Unappreciater		Blamer	
Pretender		Coercer	

DO IT ONCE, TWICE, KEEP IT GOING

Do keep in mind that as mentioned at the start of this section, your traits can and do change from project to project, day-to-day and often person-to-person. This means that when it comes to both awareness and acceptance, it is not a static process, e.g. take the test once and move on. You'll need to continually reevaluate and reassess where you were, where you are now, and where you need to be. Some might say to think of it as a marathon and not a sprint, but since I'm all about being completely honest, it's actually more like a race that never ends.

In this case though, your race is just beginning. It's time to pass the baton and onto the next section!

PART 2 – THE GREAT BOSS BUILDING BLOCKS

INTRODUCTION

Now that we've identified the bad boss traits, you may be wondering, "What's next?" Where do I go from here? That's exactly what this next part of the book is about, helping you move from awareness and acceptance to **action** – action to banish any bad boss traits you may have, and action to build (or re-build) your behaviors and skills for being a great boss.

As you read this, remember that being a bad, good, or even a great boss is not linear – you are not one or the other, there are shades of gray. The road from bad to great is fluid, dependent on your environment, how your people change, and even how you change. For example, I remember moving from managing a team of people in one country to managing my first global team. They were not only diverse from an age and gender perspective but also culturally. And they were also no longer in one office sitting alongside me, but were now spread across offices in five different countries. I guarantee that their opinions of me as a great, good, or bad boss were just as diverse. I quickly learned the importance of learning and adapting my behaviors and skills so that I could better understand and support them. And yes it took me some time to learn how to meet each of their unique needs, but one can hope I got to a place of being a good (or even great) boss to every single one of them!

THE GREAT BOSS BUILDING BLOCK™ MODEL

So what do you need to do to be a great boss? What actions can you take? To help, we're sharing with you a model we've created, called the **Great Boss Building Block** model. It's something we developed based on our own individual journeys as a boss (great, good, and bad!), and in working with and supporting others throughout our careers. It's something we truly believe can help you in your quest to be a great boss.

The model has 14 different elements, or what we're calling "building blocks." These building blocks will make up your structures, which will be individualized based on your people's needs. So the goal isn't to have *one* structure but rather to have numerous structures that are designed to help your people in the most meaningful and effective ways.

Each individual building block strengthens the structures you need to develop and maintain strong relationships with your people – ones where they're engaged, motivated, productive, and able to be their best selves. If one or more blocks are missing, your structures may not collapse, but they will be more vulnerable and less effective. Together, the blocks you choose will build resilient and lasting structures that can withstand the challenges and tests of time (and people).

And yes, we know that 14 is a big number. But rest assured, we've purposefully designed this section so that you can dip in and out to focus on one or two blocks at a time. And don't worry, we'll talk more about how to prioritize them and develop a plan later in the book. Likewise, we've also coupled the building blocks with what we associate most with the previous bad boss types. This is just a starting point though, as many of these building blocks could be useful across all the bad boss types. Keep in mind that this is a journey, a journey to be a great boss, and we're here to help you get there!

Each of the building blocks on their own could be a book, that's how important they are, and that's how much there is to say about them. For this book, however, we want to just give you a flavor of each block to help you on your journey to being a great boss. For some of you, what we're sharing will be enough and the actions and next steps will help you make that short journey to great. But if you need more, we've made sure to share our favorite and most helpful books in the acknowledgments, so do check that out for support on your great boss journey as needed!

THE GREAT BOSS BUILDING BLOCK MODEL

So here it is, the Great Boss Building Block model. As you may have noticed, there are two types of blocks. The six on the bottom, which we call the "foundation" blocks, and the eight on the top, which we call the "connecting" blocks.

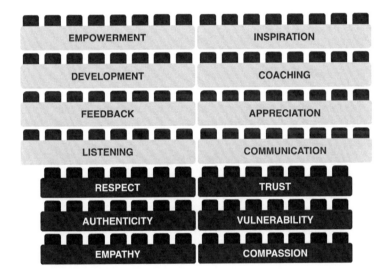

Foundation blocks

As we said, the first six building blocks are the foundation blocks. And like the foundation of any structure, they are absolutely critical as they support the weight of what's being built, ensuring it has a stable base. We affectionately call them the **"six-pack"** for two reasons. First, because, well, there are six of them. And second, because like a six-pack that some people have in their abdomen, they act to support and protect the rest of your structure, just as a six-pack does.

These six blocks represent behaviors and mindsets required to be a great boss. In the past they may have been considered "soft and fluffy," but there's no doubt about it, they're more paramount now than ever before.

When a foundation goes wrong

I'm sure you've all heard of the Leaning Tower of Pisa, which is famous for its unintended tilt. But do you know why it tilts? The construction of the Tower began like any other. The aim was for it to be a freestanding bell tower, intended to complement the Pisa Cathedral.

The building of the Tower began in 1173, but five years later they noticed that it had started to tilt. This happened for two reasons, a shallow foundation and unstable soil. But because of this, it took 100 years to complete, and it is not used as it was intended as a bell tower. The only silver lining is that it's been fighting gravity for almost 850 years and that it has turned into a money maker.

This is a great example of why it's critical to get your foundation right. To put it into our boss context, without a strong foundation, you risk your engagement and relationships with your people starting to "lean" away from what they need to be.

Connecting blocks

The second set of blocks are the eight connecting ones, which connect your people to you and your company, acting as tools to drive employee engagement and build stronger relationships. These blocks represent actions required to be a great boss and are valuable in different ways to meet the diverse needs of your people. These connecting blocks, firmly built together on top of your foundation, create a strong and enduring structure.

What we're covering

In this part of the book we will cover the following for each of the blocks:

- **Introduction** – We start out each building block with an introduction to what it is, and in some cases, how it works along with other building blocks. We also link the building blocks to the bad boss types to help you understand what these types of bad bosses may need to work on most. As noted before, this isn't black and white, as many of the building blocks are needed across *all* our bad boss types!

- **Why it matters** – Next, we talk about why this block matters to your people and your company, and the importance of getting it right. And of course, we've included lots of supporting data for those like us, who love data!

- **Actions to take** – Next, we share practical actions you can take to improve on this building block. To further guide you, we've added stories and tips to make it more relatable and actionable.

- **Next steps** – And finally, at the end of each building block we've included some steps you can take. These are meant to work alongside the actions to help you move from theory to action, taking the steps necessary to be a great boss, which is your ultimate goal!

KEY POINTS

Before we go into detailing each individual building block, here are a few key points to keep in mind:

1. **Don't wait for perfection** – First, it's important to note that your final structures don't have to be beautiful, complete, and perfect before you start using them with your people. Keep in mind that nothing will ever be perfect, making progress on individual building blocks is what truly makes a difference.

   For example, if your focus is the Appreciation block because your people have said they don't feel valued at work, you can take small steps to work toward completing this block before a formal program is put in place. You can start by doing some small acts of appreciation on your own. Maybe start each weekly team meeting with "Shout Outs," thanking individual people for the great work they had done. You'll be surprised how a small act of gratitude can have a huge impact.

2. **Order doesn't matter** – Next, although we've thought carefully about the order of the blocks in the model, most specifically which would sit next to one another, it's important not to take the placings too literally. It's not a model where you start at the bottom and work your way up, or go left to right. You need to set your own order and develop your great boss plan based on focus areas where you will make the biggest and quickest impact – remember, the enemy of progress is inertia. Please note that we'll be sharing more on how to develop your plan later in the book.

   For example, if after taking the bad boss assessment you find that you need to focus on Listening and Compassion, start with these blocks. If your people have shared with you that what they need most from you is Coaching and Development, you should probably start there. Bottom line, consider all of the building blocks that are influencing your order and come up with the order to work on the blocks that make sense for what you and your people need most.

3. **Be flexible and fluid** – We've said a few times already that things change. Whether it's the workplace, your people, or your job, nothing seems to ever stand still for long. That's why it's important to continually revisit both your structures and your priorities, focusing on blocks that are most timely and relevant. Be flexible in your approach, and open-minded to how and when you need to change your plan.

   For example, let's say you prioritize Feedback and Listening based on assessing your people's needs, and your own strengths and learning opportunities. You start the work, only to find out that the company is going to be going through a huge reorganization and you're going to have to tell people that their job is changing or layoffs are happening. You may want to shift your focus to Compassion and Communication so that you feel comfortable handling these new responsibilities.

4. **It takes practice** – There are times when you put time and effort into a building block, and it feels like an uphill battle. You read the sections, you take the actions suggested, and …. you feel like you're getting nowhere. You try it again, and again, nowhere! Well, you're not alone. When this has happened to me, I go back to two noteworthy lessons I learned when I did gymnastics.

   The first lesson is the old adage that "practice makes perfect." And that's because although some of the blocks may come more easily and naturally to you, others may not. For me, that's how I felt about anything involving twisting, which took me two or three times longer to learn than things involving flipping. I knew that eventually, I would learn it, but I had to be patient and practice it over and over again.

   As Einstein said, "Insanity is doing the same thing over and over again expecting the same results," which is my second lesson. For example, if you're working on the Feedback block, but every time you give feedback you still don't seem to get it right. Remember not to give up, but try a different approach. Talk to your people, get ideas from your peers, and find out what's working and not working, then try it again.

5. **Everyone is different** – And finally, remember that everyone is different, and one approach may work with one person, but not with another. Figure out what will work for them, and then adjust how you'll change to meet their needs.

   For example, one person on my team liked me to give feedback to them in a very direct way. "Just get to the point," they'd say to me. While another person wanted me to build up to it, and give them time to prepare for what I was going to share with them. I needed to understand this first so that I could give them what they needed.

EMPATHY

Key Building Block for the Ignorer, the Firefighter, and the Coercer

The first two building blocks are Empathy and Compassion. They're great ones to begin with as they both represent positive and altruistic traits of showing concern for others. Not a bad way to kick things off when thinking about how to be a great boss!

There are lots of ways to explain what makes them different, but to keep it straightforward, I tend to sum it up by saying that it's what they *focus on*, and their *outcome*. Starting with Empathy, it focuses on your ability to understand what another person feels. It means you can imagine yourself in their situation, with the outcome being that you feel what they must be feeling, connecting with them emotionally. On the other hand, Compassion focuses on action, taking a step to move past Empathy and asking yourself what you can do to support this person, with the outcome being to take the appropriate action(s). I like to put them together because Empathy is the fuel needed to spark Compassion, and so you need them both working together.

Another way of explaining these differences was said by the Dalai Lama:

"Picture yourself walking along a mountainous trail. You come across a person being crushed by a boulder on their chest. The empathetic response would be to feel the same sense of crushing suffocation, thus rendering you helpless. The compassionate response would be to recognize that the person is in pain, and do everything within your power to remove the boulder and alleviate their suffering."

And finally, for anyone else who like me loves a good formula, here's one that is often used to explain both the difference and intersection of these terms:

Empathy + Action = Compassion

Now that we've clarified this, let's now move our attention to the Empathy building block, digging a little deeper. We've already said that it involves you understanding another person's feelings, but what does this mean? In practice, it means that you understand their unique needs and challenges at a professional and personal level. And at the same time, you relate to their emotions, experiences, and perspectives. By doing this, you're showing them genuine care and concern, saying you value them, and in return, it builds and fosters trust and a stronger relationship.

In a world with or without empathy

Let's take a look at an example of the same situation, one with an empathetic approach and the other without:

Without empathy: A manager walks into somebody's office and says, "Hey, your numbers are down for the third quarter in a row. We've had this conversation before, and if you don't pick up your numbers in the fourth quarter, I don't know what's going to happen."

With empathy: Instead, the manager says, "We've had this conversation before, are you okay? What's going on, as I'm worried about you?"

Excerpt from a YouTube video by Simon Sinek, titled "What Empathy Looks Like"

WHY IT MATTERS

The case for empathy in the workplace has only grown in importance over the years. We've come to see the need to connect with our people at a deeper, more human level, showing empathy to support their individual and diverse needs. Empathy has become a business tool and a business imperative.

As said in a *Forbes* article, "Why Leading With Empathy Is More Important Than Ever"[28]: "We've experienced some seismic shifts in today's world. The need for deeper human connection was revealed in the pandemic. Racial and social injustice sparked dialogue about diversity, equity, and inclusion. Remote work became normalized. Remote workers fell in love with their newfound autonomy. Employees were no longer willing to tolerate being treated like a two-dimensional box on an organizational chart. As change and disruption continue at a breakneck pace, today's leaders are looking for tools to provide solid footing amid such uncertainty. A tool that is having its heyday is empathy."

Research[29] done by Catalyst on the power of empathy said that "empathy is an important driver of employee outcomes such as innovation, engagement, and inclusion – especially in times of crisis. It is a critical workplace skill that has the potential to reduce burnout and improve retention." Their data found the following:

- **Higher levels of creativity and innovation** – Employees saying their leaders were empathetic were more likely to report they were able to be creative and innovative (61% compared to only 13% with less empathetic leaders).

---

28   Alain Hunkins, Forbes, *Why Leading With Empathy Is More Important Than Ever*, 2023.

29   T. Van Bommel, Catalyst, *The power of empathy in times of crisis and beyond*, 2021.

- **Higher employee engagement** – Employees saying their leaders were empathetic were more likely to report they were engaged (76% compared to only 32% with less empathetic leaders).

- **More inclusive workplace** – Employees saying their leaders were empathetic were more likely to report their workplace was inclusive (50% compared to only 17% with less empathetic leaders).

- **Better work-life** – Employees saying their leaders were empathetic reported they are able to navigate the demands of their work and life, successfully juggling their personal, family, and work obligations (86% compared to only 60% with less empathetic leaders).

And finally, a study[30] conducted by DDI pointed to empathy as the most critical driver of overall performance. They explained that "In a leader's crucial business conversations, displaying empathy is your secret weapon. Empathic leaders naturally foster strong personal relationships and think about their team members' circumstances; they understand their challenges and frustrations, and they know that those emotions are every bit as real as their own. This helps develop perspective and opens team members to helping one another."

ACTIONS TO TAKE

As you can see, empathy can have a massive effect on your people and your business. But on the flip side, a lack of empathy can be one of the worst of the bad boss traits as it lays the foundation for others to emerge. Going back to our 10 types of bad bosses, to some extent, a lack of empathy is present in nearly all of them: The boss

---

30   Development Dimensions International, 2016.

who bailed on meetings (the Avoider), the one who never listened to ideas or suggestions (the Ignorer) and the one who said yes to project after project (the Firefighter). In all of these situations, the boss failed to empathize with their people, and in the end, failed their people!

The good news is that empathy is a skill that you can learn. So whether you're great at it, good at it, or really struggle with it, empathy can be learned and developed. These tips can help:

Open the door to empathy

One of my company values at DebCo HR is "open the door to possibilities," which reminds and guides me to be on the lookout for, aware of, and open to opportunities to deliver on my mission. The same needs to happen when it comes to empathy, because if you aren't looking for, aware of, and keeping the door "open" to times when your people need you to be empathetic, you'll completely miss opportune moments to be a more empathetic boss.

Remember that this "door," in this case, awareness, swings both ways. One way involves *your* people, being intentionally and consciously aware of what they're going through and how they're feeling. As you do this, ensure that the door is open for all of your people, and you're not just practicing "parochial empathy," which is only to show empathy to people who are similar to you, and not those who researchers call the "out-group." Keep in mind that your job as a boss is to be there for *everyone* on your team, and although being empathetic for some may be more challenging than others, it's equally as important.

The other door is being self-aware of how your emotions and behaviors are influencing those around you. The latter is something I learned the hard way, thinking that I could neatly mask and hide my emotions and that if I did, it wouldn't impact my people. Wrong! It's been proven time and time again (and I've seen it myself) that bosses who are self-aware are better able to recognize and manage their own emotions, thus not disrupting others, and more effectively reacting and supporting others when they're needed.

How do you make someone feel?

"Do you ever stop to ask yourself, 'How are you making others feel'? If not, try it now. Take a moment to look at yourself from above and replay an interaction with someone you know. Observe your body language and speech. Do you establish eye contact? Do you smile? Say hello? Are you abrupt? Not present? Quickly dismissive and do you rush on to the next part of your day?

Checking in with yourself and asking some of these questions is a great way to practice empathy and foster human connection, two qualities integral to enriching our roles as bosses and human beings traveling side by side on our journeys." *Claude Silver, Chief Heart Officer, VaynerMedia*

Seek to understand

In Brené Brown's book *Dare to Lead*, she explains that one of the signature mistakes we make when it comes to empathy is that we "believe we can take our lenses off and look through the lenses of someone else." When I read this it was one of the lightbulb moments for me. I've often believed that if I just tried hard enough, I could see things the way that others do. The problem with this is that it will never happen, for our individual lenses are shaped by our beliefs, our experiences, and everything that makes us who we are. So bottom line, we all see the world and situations differently!

But there is a bright side, for as Brown goes on to say, "What we can do, however, is honor people's perspectives as truth even when they're different from ours." It's this concept of perspective that is key. Your goal should be to seek to learn from others on your team and seek to understand their perspective. Ask questions, find out what they think, how they feel, what they're going through, etc. Create the environment for your people to share their lens with you so that you can see and understand the world that they live in.

Empathy is not jumping to conclusions, instead asking "why" – why did you say what you said, react as you did, do what you did?

Bring it home

Where do you go from here? Now that you understand your person's perspective, being open and non-judgemental in the process, are you finished? Unfortunately not, because to fully understand is to make sure that you, well, fully understand. This involves making sure that what you heard, and understood to be the truth, is accurate. This is what Brown calls the "circling back" process, and this is where you "show up with our whole hearts, pay attention, and stay curious, so we can course correct." This is where you go back and check that what you heard is actually what they meant, specifically calling attention to their point of view and perspective, by saying things such as, "What I heard you say is …", "Is this what you meant…?", or "What more do you want to share?"

The great thing about this part of the process is that it not only helps you bring it home by understanding the truth, but it gives your person the opportunity to say when you're off track. For example, they could come back and say, "Actually, that's not what I meant, I may have seemed angry or a bit pissed off, but actually I'm … "

> **"It's only when diverse perspectives are included, respected, and valued that we can start to get a full picture of the world, who we serve, what they need, and how to successfully meet people where they are."**
> — *Brené Brown, Dare to Lead*

Empathy does not mean agreement

Let us end by making one more point about empathy, addressing a common misconception which is that in order to be empathetic you need to agree with what your person says. Here's an excerpt from an Inc article by Justin Bariso, "This Brilliant 5-Word Phrase From an Ex-FBI Agent Will Help You Build Empathy and Strengthen Your Relationships" that introduces this concept:

"Chris Voss spent over two decades in the FBI, where he worked on more than 150 hostage cases and was eventually named the bureau's lead international kidnapping negotiator. Every day, Voss was forced to develop empathy for kidnappers and terrorists. If he had any chance of persuading them to give up their victims, he had to understand where they were coming from, their current state of mind, their reasons, and motivations.

Of course, he never endorsed the actions of those lawbreakers, but he worked hard to hear them out and develop understanding. They, in turn, would return the favor, giving Voss the benefit of the doubt and listening to what he had to say. This allowed Voss to save hundreds of lives over the years."

Now I'm not saying that your people will force you into hostage situations, however, there may be times when you may not agree with their rationale or reasoning. And that's okay. What is important is what we've been saying all along, which is to understand and accept what they've said as their truth so you can show them true empathy.

NEXT STEPS

☐ Assess how well you understand your people. Do you know what kind of empathetic support they require from you, or are there things that you need to learn about them first?

☐ Think back to a time when you may not have been very empathetic with one of your people. Can you remember why you weren't? Was there something you could have done differently to be more empathetic and supportive?

☐ Ask yourself, what's holding you back at times from being empathetic, and what can you do going forward to overcome these obstacles?

☐ What can you do to capture opportunities to show empathy to your people, how can you open the door to more empathetic moments?

COMPASSION

Key Building Block for the Unappreciater and the Blocker

Have you ever worked for someone who has all the traits explained under the Empathy building block, but then time and time again, still gets things wrong? They seem to genuinely understand you and your perspectives, but then nothing happens – instead, they make decisions that clearly don't put your needs first, second, or even third! That's exactly what a lack of compassion looks like. Compassion goes beyond empathy, taking a feeling and then connecting it to an action. Putting it another way, as explained in the book *Compassionate Leadership*, you "connect with empathy, and lead with compassion."

Compassion can be defined as "an empathetic emotional response to another person's pain or suffering that moves people to act in a way that will either ease the person's condition or make it more bearable[31]." It's about taking a human approach to how you lead, putting your people first by showing kindness and understanding towards them, particularly in difficult times. Compassionate bosses listen to their people and take action to support them when they face challenges or setbacks. They offer their people encouragement, and show flexibility and understanding in accommodating and supporting their personal and professional needs.

And compassion, like empathy, is not fluffy. It's being discussed even in the boardroom of companies, as shown in this excerpt of LinkedIn's former CEO and now Executive Chairman, Jeff Weiner's speech from his 2018 Wharton graduation ceremony:

---

31   Jacob Lilius et al, *What Good is Compassion at Work*, 2003.

"One of the questions I'm most frequently asked is what advice would I give my 22-year-old self? The advice I would give my 22-year-old self is to be compassionate.

I wasn't very compassionate when I was your age. As a matter of fact, I wasn't particularly compassionate until the latter stage of my career. And if it weren't for learning the meaning and value of compassion, it's likely I wouldn't be on this stage today. So that's what I'd like to talk to you about. The importance of being compassionate, and how it can change your career path, your company, and your life.

So I decided to change. I vowed that as long as I'd be responsible for managing other people, I would aspire to manage compassionately. That meant pausing, and being a spectator to my own thoughts, especially when getting emotional. It meant walking a mile in the other person's shoes; and understanding their hopes, their fears, their strengths, and their weaknesses. And it meant doing everything within my power to set them up to be successful."

WHY IT MATTERS

As with empathy, there's never been a greater need for compassion. Compassion is far from being a soft skill but is a powerhouse, a cornerstone, really, of being a great boss. When you understand through Empathy, and then lead with Compassion, you positively impact how your people both feel and act. And in return, these blocks support and drive your company's short and long-term success.

These benefits include higher levels of:

- **Creativity and innovation –** Your people are more likely to find new and improved ways of doing things if they feel they're listened to, valued, and in a safe place to present ideas.

- **Trust** – For as the expression goes, "actions speak louder than words," and through compassion, they're seeing you act in their best interest.

- **Wellbeing** – Creating a compassionate culture has been linked with lower employee emotional exhaustion and stress, meaning they can have a healthier work and social life.

And because we all love data, let's take a look at the research[32], which says that employees who work for compassionate bosses are:

- 25% more engaged in their jobs

- 20% more committed to their company

- 11% less likely to burn out

And as for bosses, the same research found that high compassion for their people versus low can lead to 66% lower stress.

ACTIONS TO TAKE

Not to be a broken record, but as we said with Empathy, Compassion, with all the good it can do, can cause difficulties when ignored or not done effectively. In fact, some of the worst bad boss stories shared with us when writing this book came from people whose boss had known the personal challenges they were facing, and then did absolutely nothing to support them. They were left devastated, with many being left with scars that took years to heal.

---

32   Rasmus Hougaard and Jacqueline Carter, *Compassionate Leadership*, 2022.

But the good news is that Compassion is a core building block that you can develop, and there are many resources out there to help with this. Here are a few of our favorite pieces of advice on learning how to be a more compassionate boss:

Lean into (and through) empathy

Since Compassion and Empathy go hand-in-hand, we suggest that you read the previous section on Empathy if you haven't already. The reason we say this is that since compassion begins by being empathetic, you need to begin by leaning into it, letting the sparks of empathy ignite your compassionate actions. This includes paying attention to your people, looking and listening to understand when things are bothering them, and when they need your help. Seeking to understand in an open-minded and non-judgemental way, hearing their truth and not yours. And, circling back to make sure you truly understand their unique perspective, so that you can swiftly and effectively be prepared to jump into compassionate action.

We highlight "leaning" in this section because great bosses need to lean into empathy and through to compassionate action. Too often bosses get their feet firmly stuck in empathy and don't *do* anything, which can sometimes be out of a lack of time, or even fear. Fear that they'll do the wrong thing, cause more problems than there were at the start, and more. Regardless of your reason for it, keep in mind as the saying goes, **"The price of inaction is far greater than the cost of making a mistake."** The problem will not go away, it will get worse, and you'll end up picking up the pieces.

To help you take this important, but difficult step, here are three tips shared in *Lead with Compassion*, where they talk about overcoming what they call the "empathetic hijack:"

1. **Take a mental and emotional step away** – Sometimes you need to step out of the emotional space to get some perspective on the situation and the person, for only with perspective will you be able to help. Keep in mind that by stepping away, *you are not stepping away from the person.* You are stepping away from the problem so you can better see it in perspective and help solve it through compassion.

2. **Coach them to find their own solution** – Being a boss is not always about solving problems for people. It is also about growing and developing your people so they are empowered and feel like they have the skills to solve their problems on their own. While it can be faster or easier to solve *for* them, it's a life-learning opportunity that people need to grow and develop. Instead, coach and mentor them to find their own answers to their challenges. Compassion will still equal action, it will just look different through this approach.

3. **Remember the power of nonaction** – It's often important to remember that sometimes people don't need your solutions. Sometimes the best way to show compassion is to be there for them, and let them know that they are heard and seen. The magic is understanding enough about the situation to know when to act and when not to act. Or, slightly tweaking William Shakespeare's line from "Hamlet" – To act or not to act: that is the question. Which is nobler, which will cause less suffering?

Light the right path

Now that you've taken the first step into compassion, it's time to check in to make sure that you're on the right "compassion path," sparked by an empathetic moment. But how do you know if you're on the right path (or, sometimes, paths)? During the empathy steps, you will have undoubtedly collected lots of information, including the details of their situation, the problems and challenges that they face, and how they are feeling. But this is not enough, as this does not directly point to one solution.

Let me share an example to illustrate this point. I had someone on my team who week after week wasn't getting their work done on time. When I asked them why this was happening (showing empathy), they explained that they were having problems at home. Their partner was putting pressure on them to help out more with the children, which was causing them stress and a lack of focus on getting their work done. This conversation lit that "empathy candle" to help me understand their problem. Now, what next? If you were in this situation, where would you go from there? Well, based on what they've told you, a few actions could come to mind such as letting them take some time off of work, changing their hours, or giving them less stressful projects to work on. But which one? You can't truly be compassionate if you pick the wrong action, and go down the right path.

What I did was ask them a couple of simple questions – "What do you need?" and "What can I do to help you improve the situation?" By asking these questions and having this dialogue, I learned more about the situation and uncovered critical information, that being a good parent *and* being challenged at work was important, but that there were times of the day when they needed to help out more at home. Armed with this, we came up with the right solutions and lit the right paths by creating a more flexible working schedule during school term time, and then normal hours outside of term time so they didn't feel pressured to be "online" during the times that their partner needed their help the most.

Continually re-light the paths

Keep in mind that compassion is an ongoing commitment, and it requires consistent effort to maintain a supportive and caring work environment. You'll need to continually go back and re-light those empathy candles and re-visit the compassion paths you've created, making sure that your actions continue to work to overcome the challenges and meet the needs of your people.

Let's go back to a story from our friend, Pat to see what happens when a boss doesn't do this:

Some years ago Pat was diagnosed with breast cancer. After enduring six months of chemotherapy, they went back to work. Their boss was both empathetic and compassionate, changing their work schedule from 9 a.m. – 5 p.m. to 8 a.m. – 4 p.m. so that Pat could attend three weeks of radiotherapy treatment. On Pat's final day of this work pattern, their boss said, "Please can you ensure you are in the office until 5:30 tomorrow as me and the rest of the team are going out with a supplier to watch horse racing, and we need to ensure someone is here to answer the phones."

This story sadly illustrates how Pat's boss not only did not act in a compassionate way but completely blew out the empathy candle! They put their needs ahead of Pat's. And by doing so, as Pat explained to me, this uncompassionate action "Completely shattered my trust and confidence in my boss and showed me the true colors of management. I decided then and there that I couldn't work for such morally indecent individuals, and left my boss and the company."

NEXT STEPS

- ☐ Ask yourself if your actions are consistent with your words. Are you moving from empathy to compassion, or do you get stuck in empathy? If you do, what's holding you back, and what can you do differently going forward?

☐ Next time you have an opportunity to show compassion to one of your people, what are you going to do to get it right? How are you going to understand what they need, and what solution will work best for them?

☐ What can you do to ensure you're constantly evolving your approach to compassion? How can you check in and adjust how you're leading with compassionate actions?

AUTHENTICITY

Key Building Block for the Pretender and the Blamer

As with the first two building blocks, the next two are similar and connected, thus they appear side-by-side in our model. That's because Authenticity and Vulnerability both focus on achieving the same goal, which is to create a sense of safety and trust for and with your people, leading to stronger collaboration, connections, creativity, and overall success. These two blocks work together to achieve these goals in different ways. Think of them as things you might "wear" as a great boss.

In this case, Authenticity is the first layer to "wear." **It's where you determine and display to others who you are, what you believe in, and what is your true self.** Vulnerability takes it to that next level, putting on that next layer to allow yourself to act in your most authentic way. It's where you reveal your *true* self, the full spectrum, including your emotions, struggles, and imperfections. This second layer is the one that is often hidden, as many of us believe that only the first layer is safe enough to show to others.

At the heart of vulnerability lies authenticity. It's what helps us uncover our true selves so that we can authentically and vulnerably "wear" all of our emotions and feelings – good and bad, perfect and imperfect.

These blocks aren't easy. They both involve courage, and not just any courage, but the courage to figure out your true self, and the courage to expose it – all of it – to others. It's about, as Brown says in *Rising Strong*, "showing up and being seen when you have no control over the outcome." So basically, courage in the face of the unknown.

This is what makes these building blocks different from all of the others. For although the others certainly require courage, it's outward courage, e.g. I'm going to courageously show Empathy, Compassion, Respect, Inspiration, etc. to my people. But with these, it's inward courage, so instead of showing *something* towards another, it's showing *yourself* to them, which is a new level of courage.

Let's now focus on Authenticity, which at its core is aligning your actions and behaviors in a way that is true to who you are (your true self) and what you believe in (your values). These become your inner compass, guiding you and showing you the way, *your* way.

Authenticity is a term and a concept that has been around for many years. Bill George, former Professor of Management Practice at Harvard Business School and ex-chairman and CEO of Medtronic, brought the concept of authentic leadership into the business world way back in 2003 in his book *Authentic Leadership.*

Since then, he's written numerous books on the topic, evolving and building on the concepts as the world around us changes and as the need for authentic leaders increases. As he and his co-author Zach Clayton explain in their most recent book, *True North: Emerging Leader Edition*, "Gen X, Millennials, and Gen Z expect different things from work and have different values, such as greater transparency and increased diversity. Whereas previous generations hesitated to openly discuss their personal lives or mental health in the workplace, emerging leaders cannot imagine closing off these parts of themselves. No longer is leadership about developing charisma, emulating other leaders, looking good externally, and acting in your self-interest."

These evolving expectations are rightfully forcing bosses to act differently to meet the needs of their people across all generations and bring that authenticity into their everyday lives, rather than keeping it hidden in a textbook.

WHY IT MATTERS

"The Boy Who Cried Wolf" is an Aesop fable that shows the importance of authenticity. It tells of a young shepherd who repeatedly raises false alarms about a wolf threatening his flock of sheep, lying to the townspeople time and time again. At first, the villagers trust the shepherd and rush to his aid to chase off the wolf. But as they come to realize that he is playing a prank on them, they trust him less and less. So much so that when the wolf really does come, they fail to respond to his cry for help, and … well, the wolf eats the sheep.

The moral of this story, as it relates to authenticity, is that if you don't tell the truth, you don't show your authentic self, your people will never follow you and never help you ward off the attacks of the "wolf."

In today's complex, evolving, and challenging world where there are different "wolves" in every corner of life, bosses need a unified team to help them "fight." But your people won't be there to help you battle the wolves if they don't believe in and trust you. This is where authenticity can help, by encouraging your people to trust and respect you, giving them the opportunity to openly express their opinions on ideas and issues. It creates an environment where your people feel it's okay for them to be authentic and vulnerable as well. Together, this has a positive effect on how the team feels, how they perform, and how you succeed in fighting off the wolves together.

Beyond a fable, recent data also shows that authenticity truly matters. The first study[33] found that authentic leadership results in **higher levels of employee engagement and satisfaction**, which talks about the positive feelings based on having an authentic leader. And

---

33   Sher Khan and Bashir Muhammad, *Effect of Authentic Leadership on Job Satisfaction and Employee Engagement*, 2021.

another study[34] found a statistically significant positive relationship between authentic leadership and **job performance**, which talks about how employees act based on authenticity.

> **"Authenticity seems to be a currency that humans have ignored for too long and at the same time the key to turning things around." — *Management 3.0, Authentic Leadership Explained***

ACTIONS TO TAKE

There are a variety of different models and books that explain how to be an authentic boss, with the most well-known being the one George describes in his first book, *Authentic Leadership*. We've pulled together some top advice from these, as well as what we've learned over the years to help you take the actions required to practice and lead in an authentic way.

Discover who you really are

In the book *True North: Emerging Leader Edition*, they say that "No one can be authentic by trying to be like someone else. You can learn from others' experience, but you cannot be successful trying to be like them." Boom! Did they hit the nail on the head or what? The journey to being authentic begins with discovering who *you* are, who is *this* person, and how they are unlike anyone else. And this can only come from self-awareness.

---

34   Frontiers in Psychology, 2021.

Being self-aware is the core foundation of authenticity. It helps you understand your vulnerabilities, your fears, your goals, what puts that spring in your step, and what keeps you up at night. By understanding and embracing both sides of your "coin," loving your weaknesses and imperfections as much as you revel in your strengths, you're on the path to being able to truly be authentic. (Hint: This leads us to the first section of the book, where you can start to be self-aware of any bad boss traits that you may have!)

Peeling back the onion

It's often hard to discover and find your true self, which is key to self-awareness. Again, we turn to George and Clayton's book, where they compare it to peeling back the layers of an onion. They describe it as follows:

"The outer layers are the ways you present yourself to the world – how you look, your facial expressions, body language, attire, and leadership style. Often these are hardened to protect you from criticism of your inner self.

Peeling the onion further, you reach your inner core where you gain a deeper understanding of your strengths, weaknesses, values, and motivations. Your inner layers feel tender and vulnerable because they have not been exposed to the scrutiny of the outside world."

"In order to find your *something more* you need a level of self-awareness that only comes from connecting with your inner voice. I call it your *emotional GPS system.*"
— *Oprah Winfrey, American talk show host, television producer, actress, author, and media proprietor*

Discover how others see you

Self-awareness, funny enough, doesn't just come from, well, you. Being self-aware has a second part, often called "external self-awareness," which involves soliciting feedback from others. This is something I learned a bit late in my journey as a boss, happening only when I had my first 360-degree feedback (a process when you go out to your team and colleagues for their feedback). At first, it was difficult and challenging to receive this feedback (stinky, really, as I think of how my own onion was peeled!), but I can honestly say that it completely changed how I approached being a boss. So much so that I turned this annual formal process into something I did informally and continuously.

To build your Authenticity block, you should solicit and welcome feedback from your people, not hide from it. See it as another way to help you be more authentic, giving you a broader and deeper understanding of who you really are. Research[35] shows that people who know how others see them are more skilled at showing empathy and taking others' perspectives. Their people also tend to have a better relationship with them, feel more satisfied, and see them as more effective in general.

But let's be truthful and say that although sometimes this feedback is positive, it is, as I mentioned earlier, at times negative. You will most likely learn of a flaw, which you should think of as an opportunity, that you may not have been aware of. A perfect example is when my team shared with me that they could tell if I agreed or disagreed with me based on how I twirled my hair. They explained that if I twirled a piece of my hair at the top of my head, it meant I disagreed with what they were saying. And if I twirled at the bottom, it meant that I agreed. Who knew? Certainly not me, and definitely something I stopped doing immediately!

---

35   Tasha Eurich, Harvard Business Review, *What Self-Awareness Really Is (and How to Cultivate It)*, 2018.

Bottom line, embrace and bring on the feedback. Use it as a way to see how others view you, their version of your true self. Is the way they see you, and the way you see you truly displaying your most authentic self?

Discover your values

So far we've been talking about one aspect of authenticity, which is what I like to call the "mirror view," so how you and others see you. The next part is deeper and more internal. It's what's in your heart, thus it's what I call your "heart view." It comes from what you believe, and don't believe in, the things you fight for and against. They're often called your personal values or your moral compass and are what lead and direct your actions, behaviors, and decisions. At home and at work, as an employee and as a boss.

Let me say there is no right or wrong set of values. As we said earlier, there is only one you, and thus your set of values will be unique to you. And, like anything else about you, they are based on who you are, your life story, and most likely will change as you and your story change.

Once you've clearly established your values, there are two things to do with them:

1. **Understand what your values mean –** Often when I ask people what their values are I find that they can clearly list them, but have difficulty explaining what they really mean. For example, they may tell me that they have a value of courage, and explain that it means not being afraid to try new things, things that scare them. Great, but what does this look like in action? To understand your own values and then describe how this affects you and your people, you can think of giving examples, like this:

My value is **Courage**.
I **show courage** by not being afraid to try new things, even if it might scare me.
At work, **I show courage** by embracing innovation and being there to hear far-fetched ideas from my team that could help our business.
My team can **show me courage** by openly sharing ideas on how to grow the business, no matter how crazy the idea might sound.

2. **Set your values boundaries –** Once you're clear on what they mean, it's time to be clear on what they *don't* mean, the flip side. By doing this you can set boundaries that set clear limits for you and your people on what can and cannot be done. For example, going back to the value of courage just mentioned, does this mean that you expect people on your team to be innovative at all times? Only when you are establishing new processes or products? When and how?

As explained in *True North: Emerging Leader Edition*, "If moral values inform the positive principles you live by, ethical boundaries set absolute limits on your actions. You will encounter many gray areas in life and work. Where do you draw the line between the actions that are acceptable and those that are not? What lines will you refuse to cross?" If you are going to be authentic, and use this as a way to support your people and set them up for success, you must set these boundaries, and then make sure that your people are absolutely clear on what they are.

Bring your authentic self "out to play"

Now that you've figured out what you're being authentic about, the next step is to go out and, well, be authentic. I'd like to say that this is easy, and while at times it is, there are other times, especially when things get tough, that it can be difficult to do. But it is absolutely critical to "bring them out to play," as I describe it, turning them from words to actions.

Here are three things to keep in mind in bringing your authentic self "out to play."

1. **Be transparent** – Throughout the book, we'll talk about and encourage transparency, from how you communicate to your people to how you give feedback and appreciation, transparency is a cornerstone of being a great boss. The same is absolutely true when it comes to authenticity, for quite frankly, you can't be seen as authentic if your people don't see you openly and transparently living your authentic self.

   There are two parts to this transparency. The first is in *what you say*, where you openly and honestly share your thoughts and beliefs. This helps your people understand what you stand for so that they can align their work to meet these expectations. We mentioned this earlier when we talked about values boundaries, and the same is true with all aspects of your true self. Open the door and let your people see your true self. Don't hide behind doors, expecting them to guess what you think and believe in. This is when mistakes and problems happen.

   The second part of transparency has to do with *your actions*. It's critical to be consistent and reliable in how you live your true self. You can't one day say that you believe and value one thing, and the next day say the opposite, or else you risk confusion, frustration, and again, mistrust amongst your team. I know this from experience as I once had a boss who said that they valued courage and innovation, saying it was something we should always strive for. And some days they did, applauding us when we presented new ideas and other days they'd berate us for wasting time with "lamebrained" ideas. The overall message was confusing, and eventually, we stopped contributing new ideas.

2. **Be intentional** – Another thing we talk a lot about in this book is the concept of being intentional, committing yourself to what you are trying to achieve. And when it comes to authenticity, this is absolutely critical so that you can get great benefits for yourself, your people, and your company from being authentic. When explaining this in leadership workshops I often start by asking this question, "Why would you have beliefs and values if you aren't going to use them?" It's like having tools in your garden shed that gather dust, instead of using them to help you create and maintain a beautiful garden.

   Use your beliefs and values as a roadmap, a compass, tools – whatever you want to call it – to make decisions. Use them to regulate your attitudes, behaviors, and actions. This will help you stay authentic in good times and bad, not taking the easy route and straying away from your true self. And yes it may be hard, especially when you get pressure from others, but remind yourself why you have them to begin with.

3. **Be balanced** – As a gymnast, balance was absolutely critical, it's what kept me safe and what helped me perform at my best. And, guess what, the same is true with authenticity. With authenticity, you need to balance a few things. The first is balancing how authentic you are going to

be. This is something we cover with the next building block, Vulnerability, talking about how you need to decide based on the person and situation how vulnerable you are going to be. With Authenticity, the same is true, as there are times when you might want to hold it back. Let's use the value and belief of "innovation" to bring this to life. Say you have someone on your team who is still learning the basics, and although you want them to be innovative, they're just not ready for this. The last thing you want to do is challenge them on this, making them feel uncomfortable and possibly incompetent by forcing your values on them. So you hold back until the time is right.

The next is related, and is about balancing your authenticity with the various needs of your people and your business, leading with both heart and mind. Let's continue with the value of innovation. I've been in situations with my people and other business leaders where I need to quietly tuck this away as it's just not appropriate. One example is when we were in the middle of a business crisis and just surviving was the goal, or when we already had too many new ideas that we were working on and couldn't handle another, or when we didn't have the money to do anything innovative. The bottom line is: Don't put your authenticity above the needs of others. They need to be "brought out to play" at the right time and in the right place.

"Just listen to your gut, and on the way down to your gut, check in with your heart. Between those two things, they'll let you know what's what."
— *Ted Lasso, Ted Lasso television show*

NEXT STEPS

☐ The journey to authenticity begins with self-awareness. Invest time in doing an audit of your strengths, weaknesses, values, and motivations, peeling back all layers of your "onion," your true self.

☐ Ask yourself, "How am I showing up today?" Do you like who you are, and do you feel like you're modeling your authentic self, including core values and behaviors? If not, how can this be changed?

☐ How can you lead in an authentic way, consistently doing so as you deal with different people and different types of work?

VULNERABILITY

Key Building Block for the Avoider, the Hoarder, and the Coercer

I'm embarrassed to say this, but early in my career as a boss I got it all wrong when it came to Vulnerability. I thought that being vulnerable was a sign of weakness and that I would be judged if I was vulnerable, if I revealed my true self, including my emotions, struggles, and imperfections to my people. I thought the rewards were not worth the risks, for being vulnerable would lead to me not being respected, trusted, and being seen as a strong and competent boss. Why did I believe this? Well, probably because this is what I had been told time and time again by my bosses. Sound familiar?

Let me start by saying that being vulnerable is not wrong. In fact, being vulnerable is very right! **It is not a weakness, but a strength, showing that you have the courage to authentically express who you really are in front of and to others.** The courage to remove or unzip your armor that's protecting (and hiding) you from others is a risk, yes, but it's a smart risk. One that shows your people that you are human, emotionally exposing and opening yourself up to them. And by doing this, you can create a sense of safety and trust, leading to stronger collaboration, connections, creativity, and success.

> **"Perfect and bulletproof are seductive, but they don't exist in the human experience. We must walk into the arena, whatever it may be, with courage and the willingness to engage. Rather than sitting on the sidelines and hurling judgment and advice, we must dare to show up and let ourselves be seen. This is vulnerability. This is daring greatly." — *Brené Brown, Daring Greatly***

Vulnerability in action

In 2008, at the height of the recession, Howard Schultz returned to his former role as CEO at Starbucks. The coffee chain was going through a rough patch, with more than 600 Starbucks stores closing their doors, and with subsequent layoffs of approximately 12,000 employees.

Schultz stood in front of his workforce and emotionally shared with them the message that if the company does not change, Starbucks as a company will be no more. His openness, transparency, and allowing himself to be vulnerable to connect with his employees, resulted in Starbucks' recovery, cementing their status as one of the best brands in the world.

As Schultz said when explaining his actions, "I think one of the most undervalued characteristics of leadership is vulnerability and asking for help. When you're vulnerable and ask for help, people come towards you. I've tried to do that every step of the way and be honest and truthful about what I know, what I don't, and most importantly, what I believe."

WHY IT MATTERS

It doesn't seem that long ago that vulnerability was not only discouraged but not even spoken about. But as the world around us changes, throwing us challenge after challenge, what I can say is that honesty, transparency, and, now, vulnerability are frequently part of the conversation and seen as fundamental business imperatives. And with new generations entering the workforce, ones who share their every emotion, action, and challenge, vulnerability is now an expectation and a necessity.

There are numerous benefits of vulnerability to keep in mind. If you're asking yourself, "Is it worth it to be vulnerable?" here are just a few results of being vulnerable:

- **Makes you more relatable –** As a boss, there are times when we need our people to look up to us, and, in essence, be "above" them. And while this is important, to have a strong connection with them, at times you also need to sit side-by-side with them. Vulnerability can help with this, as it helps your people relate to you and see you as another human. Or, as my former CEO used to say, "see that you put your trousers on one leg at a time."

- **Builds trust –** Another key element of being a great boss is Trust, which is unsurprisingly another building block. Vulnerability is an area that can help your people trust you, for it shows them that you care enough to be authentic and open up to them, creating a safe environment where they in turn can do the same.

- **Drives innovation –** This safe environment created through vulnerability also encourages your people to more freely and openly share their ideas, which is where the magic of innovation happens. They're more likely to come up with creative solutions, creating a culture of experimentation, where failure is seen as an opportunity for growth and learning.

- **Creates resilience –** And finally, in order for you and your team to be able to deal with all that life throws our way both at work and at home, resilience is absolutely necessary. By being vulnerable and creating that culture of vulnerability, you and your people will be more open about how to deal with setbacks when life knocks you down. How can you work together to pick yourselves up and get on with things?

> ## It takes less time and energy to be vulnerable
>
> Let me ask you a question. Isn't it exhausting to hide your true self? To sock away your vulnerabilities so no one thinks you're "fragile"? Constantly wearing these masks that we have to put on and off, remembering when best to wear them, understanding what they all mean … It's exhausting!
>
> Well, research shows that those masks might not even be necessary. Did you know that it **takes only eight seconds of discomfort to get through the nervous energy that forms when you are getting ready to be vulnerable**? How quickly you can feel relief from the anxiety! Now compare that with the amount of time and mental energy you spend when you let the thoughts stir around in your head, ruminating on what to do with them. The hours and days add up, don't they? So I ask you another question, would you prefer eight seconds, days, or weeks?

ACTIONS TO TAKE

Let's not sugarcoat it, being vulnerable is not easy. In fact, it can be terrifying. And that's because putting yourself out there can be scary and uncomfortable no matter how confident and self-assured you are. It involves taking risks, taking chances, and walking into the unknown.

However, on the flip side, we know that there are many benefits of vulnerability. And yes, it takes courage and bravery to be vulnerable, to open the door and remove the walls we've built to protect ourselves when there is no guarantee of what is on the other side. Will it be safe? Will we face challenges, maybe even opposition? But it's well worth it. In fact, when I've taken that first step it's felt like a weight has been lifted, thinking to myself, "Why didn't I do this sooner?" So, as Simon Sinek said in his book *Leaders Eat Last*, you need to **"Embrace the discomfort and use it as an opportunity for growth and learning."**

With that being said, there are some practical actions that you can take to embrace and open the door to your Vulnerability building block. The starting point is to begin with Authenticity, remembering that it is the first layer you need to put on if you're going to "wear" vulnerability well.

Check your ego at the door

We can't talk about vulnerability without addressing something we all have, our ego. It's what helps protect your self-image and self-worth. Sometimes, though, your ego can get in the way, jumping in to protect you when you feel threatened, embarrassed, ashamed, etc. And when this happens, your ego overrides what actually may be happening, coming up with a false reality.

I love how Brown explains this in her book *Dare to Lead*: "I think of my ego as my inner hustler. It's that voice in my head that drives pretending, performing, pleasing, and perfecting. The ego loves gold stars and craves acceptance and approval. Our ego will do almost anything to avoid or minimize the discomfort associated with feeling vulnerable or even being curious, because it's too risky."

For example, let's say a member of your team challenges your suggestion on how they should do something with ideas and concepts that you are not familiar with. You feel embarrassed as you're not clear and comfortable with their ideas. And you feel threatened as you believe they're questioning your knowledge and your authority. Your ego, your "inner hustler," takes over your thoughts, creating a false reality that leads you to become defensive and put up walls.

Let's now look at this situation without your ego, putting it aside and leaving it at the door. Instead, you are vulnerable, asking your employee to explain more about their ideas. The result is that they feel listened to and valued for their contributions, and you, as a boss, will learn something new, as there are now two people working on the problem at hand. The end result? You'll put something in place that was much better than what you, alone, had suggested in the first place. Boom, how's that ego?!

Ask for help

I have this friend who is the queen of asking for help. Whether it's letting her dogs out into the garden when she's stuck at work, picking up something for her when you're at the shops, or putting her trash cans out when she's away on vacation. And I admit I used to judge her for always asking for help. That was until I realized that by asking for help and wearing her vulnerability "crown," she was actually quite smart. By asking for help, she ensured that things got done, and she showed me that I was valued as a friend by asking for my help. Genius!

The same is true in the workplace, where too often as bosses we don't ask for help (I raise my hand to that). We see it as a sign of weakness doing so, thinking that surely people will judge me if I can't handle things on my own, and surely I should have all the answers. Wrong!

> **"Weak leaders hesitate to ask for help, fearing others will see them as incapable. Strong leaders, on the other hand, focus on more strategic issues of accomplishing the mission, developing team capabilities and confidence, and gaining buy-in for overall success."**[36]
> — *Dianna Booher, author*

Asking for help is actually a superpower. All this with five simple words and a punctuation mark – *can you please help me?* Help me get work done. Help me come up with new ideas. Help me overcome a

---

36   Dianna Booher, Forbes, *How Strong Leaders Ask For Help*, 2018.

challenge. Help me deal with a difficult customer. The list goes on and on. In fact, once you open the floodgates, you'll wonder why you didn't think of asking for help sooner. Asking for help makes you more productive, efficient, and innovative while fostering a culture of collaboration. Plus, as my friend showed me, it makes your people feel *valued* that you want (and need!) their help.

Own your mistakes

Have you ever made a mistake at work that makes you cringe to this day? Whether it's a newly hired trainee who points out a mistake you've made in a presentation you've been staring at for three weeks, or realizing that you forgot to deliver on a critical task? Well, it happens to the best of us. Even if you're good or great at your job, human beings are prone to making mistakes.

But society and business have trained us that admitting to imperfections is bad and should be avoided. You can see this all the time watching others scurry for cover when a mistake is made (remember the Blamer boss?). They do this by gleefully shaming those unfortunate enough to have had a mistake exposed. They point their fingers and crow loudly that the mistake transcends all others, secretly joyful and relieved that their mistakes were not noticed. But as Robert F. Kennedy once said, "Only those who dare to fail greatly can ever achieve greatly." Or to put it another way, as Eleanor on the television show *The Good Place* said, "Pobody's Nerfect."

If you need proof of this, just search for stories of failure to success. Here are a few: former president Abraham Lincoln experienced failure in his first businesses. Michael Jordan, one of the all-time greatest basketball players, was not only cut from his high school team but missed more than 9,000 shots in his career, and lost almost 300 games. And Oprah Winfrey, talk show host, television producer, actress, and author, was fired from an early job as a television news anchor. They've all made mistakes and all moved on to be very successful, proving the power of mistakes, and how they can even end up being a net positive in the long run.

As a boss, you need to be vulnerable and brave enough to own your mistakes and to admit when you've made them. Start seeing mistakes as a strength and not a weakness, and start having the courage to own any that you make in front of your people. And when I say own them, I mean *really* own them, talk about them, dissect them, and turn them into learning moments for your entire team by discussing what you've all learned through them. If you do this it will create a safe environment, that "circle of safety" as Sinek calls it, where others will openly admit and discuss their mistakes. It shows your people that you're human and that you value honesty and transparency. It creates a culture of accountability, where team members are more likely to take responsibility for their own mistakes. And it creates an environment of respect, trust, and engagement leading to a high-performing, trustworthy team.

A social approach to mistakes

To encourage their employees to speak up and embrace their mistakes, one company I spoke to set up a "Yeah, we failed" Slack social channel. By doing this, people could openly own their mistakes, and at the same time, others could learn from them so that they didn't make the same one. Now that's creating a culture of owning up to your mistakes and learning from them!

Get the balance right

Let me end by dispelling a myth about vulnerability, which is that it is all about *full disclosure*, meaning you have to tell everything and leave nothing unsaid. Think of it like spices in cooking, where you need to add the right amount to get the right result. This is the same as with vulnerability, getting the balance right by not oversharing when it's not necessary to help move towards your or your team's goals.

For example, at a previous company, we had made the decision to move our offices from the suburbs to the city. We briefed our managers and asked them to explain to their people the rationale for this, and then discuss what support they'd need if they decided to move with the company. I remember an employee coming up to me afterward to complain about their boss, telling me that they had been forced to listen to them go on and on about how they weren't sure how they would manage to get their children into a new private school and worrying about finding a new house. The employee said to me, "Did they not see that their problems were so far from my problems? I have no children, and there is no way I could afford to buy, let alone rent, in the city." This example shows that although the boss was being vulnerable, sharing that they too would have challenges with the move, in this situation they overshared. This is also where Empathy and Compassion could have also been shown, showing support and understanding for what their employee was going through.

In Brown's book *Dare to Lead*, she describes this as setting boundaries. Explaining how it's important to set boundaries when it comes to vulnerability, making it clear as to what's okay and what's not okay, and why. From my experience, the key to this has to do with reading your audience (your people) and the situation. Ask yourself, how much vulnerability is right for each of my people? Are they comfortable with it, so I can let it flow freely, or does it make them uncomfortable, so I need to tread carefully when I behave in this way? Does the situation warrant a lot of vulnerability, or like in the example, is it best to be supportive and let my employee be vulnerable? Bottom line, there is no right or wrong answer, no manual that says to be 100% vulnerable in one situation and for one person, and only 75% vulnerable in another situation or for another person. You need to clearly and intentionally understand and draw the boundaries for each person and each situation.

Vulnerability minus boundaries is not vulnerability. It's confession, manipulation, desperation, or shock and awe, but it's not vulnerability." — *Brené Brown, Dare to Lead*

NEXT STEPS

☐ Think back to a time when you didn't admit that you'd made a mistake, or if you couldn't handle a situation. What was your reason for doing this? What impact did this have on you and others?

☐ Ask yourself, what stops you from showing vulnerability? Is it you? Your people? The company? List out these reasons and these barriers, and then list out what you can do to remove them.

☐ What can you do going forward to be more vulnerable, and are there certain situations or opportunities for you to act in this way?

RESPECT

Key Building Block for the Ignorer, the Firefighter, and the Coercer

Well, we've come to the final two of the foundational building blocks, our six-pack. And like the others sitting side-by-side to one another in the model, Respect, and Trust are related and connected, relying and depending on one another. However, there are two key things that make them different from all of the other building blocks.

The first difference is the **dependencies** that Respect and Trust have with the other building blocks throughout the model. While others to some extent rely on a few of the other blocks (e.g. Compassion depends on Listening, Vulnerability on Feedback, Appreciation on Authenticity), Respect and Trust pretty much depend and rely on *all* of the other building blocks. For example, you show respect by listening to your people, giving them feedback, being empathetic to them, etc. You show trust by coaching them, showing them appreciation, being vulnerable, etc. You get the idea: Respect and Trust both **depend on and inform** the actions of the other building blocks to happen.

The next difference has to do with the direction that they need to flow. For Respect and Trust, they **have to flow in two directions** – you need to respect and trust your people *and* hope that they respect and trust you in return. This means that even if you show respect and trust to your people, they might not show them back to you. To illustrate this, think of a time when you had a boss who *you* just didn't respect and trust. Even if they treated you with respect and trust, it would make no difference because they got other building blocks wrong, and because of this, it affected your own trust and respect for them. Both respect and trust originate with you as the boss. While the other blocks *can*, and, in an ideal world, *would* flow in both directions, too, that's not usually the case.

Now that we've looked at the differences, let's now take a step back and explain respect and trust, two words that are often used interchangeably, but are indeed different. At a high level, they differ in regard to their beliefs. Respect is **believing in the value of a person**, and trust is **believing that they'll do the right thing**.

Drilling down a bit deeper, respect involves feelings of admiration towards someone. You recognize their value, abilities, and contributions, and treat them with dignity and courtesy. You're willing to listen to their different opinions and perspectives without judging or criticizing them, and you treat them with kindness and consideration, showing interest in their thoughts and feelings. On the other hand, trust is the belief or confidence in the honesty, integrity, and reliability of someone. When you trust someone, you believe that they will act in your best interest and do the right thing, making you feel safe and secure with them.

Can you have one without the other? Can you respect someone without trusting them? Can you trust someone you don't respect? Great questions, and ones that we're asked all the time, in and outside of work. For example, in choosing an electrician to support with a building project, we asked our contractor to recommend electricians to us. They explained how they have several electricians who they respect, ones they know will do good work as they are highly skilled. However, they only have a few that they trust, meaning ones that they would want to bring in because they trust not only the end work but also how they will behave throughout the process. Factors like doing the work on time and to cost, and keeping any agreed-upon commitments. For our contractor, this is more important in their decision-making, with trust overshadowing respect.

What really matters in all of this isn't whether you have one without the other, because it can depend on your situation, but rather understanding how **respect and trust work together and how they co-exist. This is where the magic happens.** And as shared in a blog[37] by Julia Felton, this is where 1+1=3 ... meaning that together they can achieve so much more!

Respect versus fear

There's one more thing we'd like to say about respect before we move on, and it's based on a conversation we had as we were writing this section. As we went through our years as bosses, we shared what we thought our people would say if we asked them if they had respected us. I made the comment that most of the time I felt that they did, but other times I may have confused it with fear (during my micromanager years, I'm embarrassed to say). This was such an ah-ha moment for me and one that you may have experienced.

The point and the question you should ask yourself is – **do your people look *up* to you or do they look *out* for you coming?** Fear or respect? As Garry Ridge, Chairman Emeritus WD-40 Company explained about fear, "It is one of the most disabling behaviors we have, it can stop your people in their tracks. Think of a deer standing in the road, why don't they move, because they are afraid. This is the last thing you want for your people, paralyzed by fear."

WHY IT MATTERS

Showing genuine and meaningful respect to your people can deliver enormous benefits and returns. And that's because employees who feel respected are more satisfied with their jobs, more motivated, and more loyal to you and your company. They're also, as Associate Professor Kristie Rogers[38] from Marquette University explained, "more resilient, cooperate more with others, perform better and more creatively, and are more likely to take direction from their leaders."

---

37   Julia Felton, *Trust and Respect Make Great Partners*.

38   Kristie Rogers, Harvard Business Review, *Do Your Employees Feel Respected?*, 2018.

A global study[39] conducted by Christine Porath, professor at Georgetown University's McDonough School of Business, found that respect was ranked as the most important leadership behavior. The study also found positive impacts of respect on both employees and the business, supporting what we said earlier. Respondents who felt respected reported 56% better health and wellbeing, 89% more enjoyment and job satisfaction, and 92% greater focus and prioritization.

On the flip side, a lack of respect can cause severe damage. As explained in *Crucial Conversations*, "**Respect is like air. As long as it's present, nobody thinks about it. But if you take it away, it's all that people can think about**." Supporting this, the study also found that 80% of employees treated disrespectfully lost time worrying about the situation, and ruminating on the bad behavior, 48% deliberately cut back or reduced their efforts, and 12% left their job.

---

39   Christine Porath, *Cycle to Civility*, 2016.

Is respect the *secret sauce* for employee engagement?

Another thing that matters for every boss and at every company is employee engagement, something we mention throughout the book. From motivation to productivity to wellbeing, the impact of engagement is both wide and deep.

I read an interesting blog[40] where they showed the correlation between the 12 employee engagement questions asked through the Gallup survey and respect. It shows how so many of the factors impacting engagement have a direct link and relationship to respect. Here are a few examples to bring this to life:

Survey question: Do you know what is expected of you at work? This question relates to respect, being clear with your people about what is expected of them to show that you respect them enough to put the time and energy into sharing these expectations. It signals that you care about them succeeding, and will support them with this.

Survey question: Do you have the materials and equipment to do your work right? This question again has a link to respect as by giving your people the materials and equipment to do their job it shows that you respect them by setting them up for success. I actually heard of an employee leaving their company after their first day because their boss hadn't given them supplies, specifically pens and pencils. When I conducted the exit interview with this employee they said to me that if their boss didn't respect and care about them on day one, how would they be on day two, 22, 32, etc.? They didn't want to stick around long enough to know!

And finally, respect is important because it serves as the bedrock, the foundation, on which trust is grown. Without respect, trust, its true partner, will wither and die. Scary, right?

---

40 Mary Dunn, LinkedIn, *Is Respect the Secret to Employee Engagement?*, 2019.

ACTIONS TO TAKE

The good news with Respect is that as you get stronger with the other building blocks, it will contribute to you getting stronger as it relates to respect. For example, the better you get at Compassion, the more respect you will receive from your people, the better you get at Listening, the more respect you will receive from your people.

The bad news is that unfortunately, it doesn't end there. Respect isn't automatically given just because you're great at the other building blocks, rather it's earned. And then, once you've earned it, it's an ongoing process to hold onto this valuable commodity. But of course, we're here to share some actions to take to create a free-flowing culture of respect. Let's get to it…

Start by giving respect

I'm sure you've heard many times before that as a boss it all starts with you. As a boss (*the* boss), you need to take that first step and role model something before your people will follow suit. Well, this is also true to earn respect, for you must first give respect before it's given back to you. You can't disrespect others, and then think that they will respect you – it just won't happen. Because respect flows in both directions, to earn it, you need to give it, and so on, and so on.

For some of your people, you may already respect them, and that's great. For others whom you do not respect, you need to ask yourself if there's a particular reason they don't have your respect. Is it because you don't really know them, so you can't value what they have to offer? Or you haven't seen them in action, so you don't know what contributions they've made or can make in the future? Was it something they've said or done in the past, so your respect for them needs to be rebuilt? Again, *giving* respect is critical, so you want to get to the bottom of why you're struggling.

Let's pause for a moment and point out something that is overlooked or ignored, that there are two types of respect, and therefore two ways to earn it. As defined by Rogers[41] they are:

- **Owed respect** – This is given equally to everyone. It meets the universal need to feel included and valued.

- **Earned respect** – This is given to people who display valued qualities or behaviors. It distinguishes employees who have exceeded expectations and, particularly in knowledge work settings, affirms that each employee has unique strengths and talents. Earned respect meets the need to be valued for doing good work.

We point this out as too often we've seen bosses focus on the latter, earned respect, dismissing the need to give owed respect as well. When this happens, you create an imbalance, which can frustrate your people and drive the wrong actions and behaviors. As Rogers says, "Workplaces with low owed respect but high earned respect can encourage excessive competition among employees. It could hinder people from sharing critical knowledge about their successes and failures, and it often promotes cutthroat, zero-sum behavior." The key is to get the balance right, freely and fairly giving both owed and earned respect to your well-deserving people.

Remove the barriers that block respect

There are other things that get in the way of respect, barriers that prevent it from being given in a *fair, consistent, and inclusive* manner. In Scott's book *Radical Respect*, she breaks these down into three root causes, explaining them as follows:

---

41   Kristie Rogers, Harvard Business Review, *Do Your Employees Feel Respected?*, 2018.

1. **Bias**: *Not meaning it* – Bias, which is often called unconscious bias, comes from the part of our mind that jumps to conclusions, usually without our even being aware of it. These conclusions and assumptions aren't always wrong, but they often are, especially when they reflect stereotypes.

2. **Prejudice**: *Meaning it* – Sometimes we rationalize our biases and they harden into prejudices. In other words, we justify our biases rather than challenge their flawed assumptions and stereotypes.

3. **Bullying**: *Being mean* – The intentional, repeated use of in-group status or power to harm or humiliate others. Sometimes bullying comes with prejudice, but often it's a more instinctive behavior. There may be no thought or ideology at all behind it.

We point these out so that you don't let these barriers get in the way of you respecting *all* of your people. Give every member of your team – no matter the job level, experience, background, etc. – an equal chance to earn your respect. To see them for who they are, and what they have to offer and contribute.

Equally important, as a boss you need to hold your people to the same standards. Scott talks about using courage to challenge and remove these barriers, taking action and putting in place consequences so you can create and maintain a working environment that "eliminates bad behaviors and reinforces collaborative, respectful behavior."

Commit to respect

One of the things that makes respect so challenging is how frail it is. How it can be lost so quickly, often when you least expect it, and in ways that you may never have imagined. For example, what does it say to your people when you cancel a meeting at the last minute?

Or if you schedule a 15-minute meeting and have it run for an hour? Does it say that you respect them, or does it say that you don't value and respect them and their time? How about when you overload them with work? Or the opposite, leave them waiting for you to give them something to do? Again, does it say respect or disrespect to your people?

Respect is shown in what you say (and don't say) and do (and don't do). From small to large behaviors and actions, individually and collectively they show your people whether or not you respect them.

If you want to hold on to your people's respect, you need to commit to taking actions that will drive it. You need to *consciously, intentionally, and consistently* act in ways that will shout from the rooftops that you respect them, leaving no doubts in their minds.

One route to achieve this is through your other building blocks, paying attention to the ones that drive and support Respect. Here are two examples:

- **Listening –** To feel respected, your people need to feel that they are heard. And to be heard, well, you need to actively listen. If your people do not feel that they have a voice, that this voice is listened to, and that their words will inspire action, respect will never happen. When we reach the Listening building block, you'll learn that your people need to know that what they say to you is important, that you value their input, and that you care and respect them enough to listen to them.

- **Compassion –** If you recall, compassion is about taking a humanistic approach to how you lead, showing kindness and understanding towards them, particularly in difficult times. Showing compassion is the epitome of respect, putting your people and their needs first, and showing them that *they* really matter, not just their work.

Another critical way of showing your commitment to respect is your follow-through, which I'll explain using a sports analogy. In baseball, when you follow through you swing the bat as you hit the ball. And by doing this, you increase the time that the ball is in contact with the bat, ultimately affecting the force of your hit. Hit the ball harder, and your team is more likely to win.

With respect, instead of swinging a bat, your follow-through is doing what you say you'll do. Let's go back to Pat's story about breast cancer treatment. Pat's boss was at first respectful of their needs, giving them time off for treatment. But then out of the blue, their boss told Pat that they were needed to come into the office to cover the phones while the team was out with a supplier, meaning that Pat couldn't make their treatment. This left Pat shocked and frustrated, completely eliminating any respect that Pat had for their boss, respect they had built up over the many months of treatment. What a shame! So remember how crucial it is to keep your word, do what you say you'll do, and follow through. From the small to the big actions, this can be the difference between keeping and losing respect, or going back to baseball, striking out, or hitting a home run!

NEXT STEPS

- [ ] Assess how strong Respect is between you and your people now. Are there gaps in where it is now and where it needs to be going forward? If so, how can you improve it based on the tips and actions shared?

- [ ] Assess the various ways that you are showing respect to your people now that have been effective. What else can you do in the future to increase and improve respect? Can it be more consistent?

☐ Consider what you can do to ensure that there are no barriers in place that prevent your team from respecting one another. Are there things you could do to drive a more inclusive culture, where differences are valued and respected? How is your balance of owed and earned respect amongst your team?

TRUST

Key Building Block for the Hoarder and the Micromanager

And here we are at Trust, the final of the six-pack building blocks, the one that sits and works alongside Respect. It is the belief or confidence in the honesty, integrity, and reliability of someone. **When you trust your people and they trust you, you have this belief that they will act in your best interest and do the right thing, making you feel safe and secure with them.** Together, Trust and Respect are a powerful duo, achieving things that other building blocks cannot do.

But there are also some things that only trust can do, as it has stronger powers than even respect. And that's because as said by Dr. Kathy Allen, "**Trust is both the glue that holds relationships together and the grease that helps us get things done**." And although trust's counterpart, respect, has an important role to play by opening the door to relationships with your people, only trust can fully get them in.

> "**A relationship with no trust is like a cell phone with no internet. All you can do is play games.**" — *Ken Blanchard and Randy Conley, Simple Truths of Leadership*

Another difference between Respect and Trust, and in fact Trust and any other of the building blocks, is something that Stephen R. Covey calls an "emotional bank account." In his book *The 7 Habits of Highly Effective People*, he uses this metaphor to describe the concept of an emotional, or trust, bank account. When you act in a trustworthy way, you make a "deposit." When you act to the contrary, you make a "withdrawal." The aim here is to stay in credit. This is useful because as humans we're bound to slip up, mistakes are bound to happen, and they're a natural part of growth. But because we have "money" (trust) in our account, these missteps are accepted, we're cut some slack, and we can bounce back, make things right, and continue to have a solid and trusting relationship.

I can remember this happening to me, working for a boss whom I had the utmost trust for, and who had "credit" in my trust account. He called me late one night to say that he couldn't appear on a live TV interview the next morning and needed me to drop everything and do it on their behalf. I could have gotten angry, I could have said no (especially as I had never done anything like this before), but because they had this credit I agreed. And the interesting thing about this example is that even though he "spent credit" from the trust account for what he had asked me to do, I actually put some back in because I felt so trusted that he had thought of me to take his place. So one deposit and one withdrawal!

On the flip side, when there is no trust in the bank account, things can get a bit hairy. Take for example, what I refer to as the "chair incident" story. Years ago, I was asked to present to a group of employees at one of my company's sites some good news, a new employee benefit. When I had announced this at other sites, I was met with a standing ovation and lots of happy, smiling faces. But at one site, instead of applause, I was met with rows of employees standing up with their chairs in their hands, yelling at me to leave. Quite a difference! Well, I finished my talk and got off the stage as quickly as I could to find the site manager to explain their reaction to me. They apologized and said that they should have warned me that at this site there was no trust whatsoever. So although what I was saying was something positive, these employees had nothing in their "trust bank" to even give me a chance!

As you can see from these stories, trust changes everything. A lack of trust can destroy a good thing, but when it's there it has the potential to build amazing success.

People come with trust baggage

After having my bad boss, the one who led me to come up with the phrase "bad bosses ruin lives," I was quite frankly damaged. I was no longer the confident and trusting professional I had been before, but an insecure and mistrusting one. And this is who my next boss had to deal with and manage.

For my boss, it meant starting the trust "race" way before the starting line. So before she could even convince me to earn her trust, she had to build me up and get me to the starting line. Which, by the way, she did brilliantly.

I say this to make the point that our people come with baggage. Whether they've had a bad boss, a great boss, or anything in between, they come with their experiences and expectations, and … we need to learn to deal with them! In this particular situation, my poor boss had a harder battle, but for previous bosses, I came ready and willing to trust them from the start. The key is to find out what baggage the person has, and figure out how best to deal with it, carry it, and get them past the starting line to continue your "race"!

WHY IT MATTERS

According to the Edelman Trust Institute, an organization that has been surveying trust for more than 20 years, **trust is the ultimate currency**. "Trust is the foundation that allows an organization to take responsible risk, and, if it makes mistakes, to rebound from them. For a business, especially, lasting trust is the strongest insurance against competitive disruption, the antidote to consumer indifference, and the best path to continued growth. Without trust, credibility is lost and reputation can be threatened."

And in the complex and challenging world we work, and lead, in, if we ever needed currency, if we ever needed trust, it would be now! Sinek said in *Leaders Eat Last*, **"While inspiration gets people to**

take the first step and follow in the calm, trust gets people to climb the hill and brave the storm." And as I'm sure you'd agree, we have had our fair share of storms lately, and the "weather" doesn't seem to be improving!

Trust in a hybrid world

Remote and hybrid work have emerged as the new reality for organizations around the world. How can you reap the benefits of these new ways of working? The answer comes down to one crucial element – you guessed it: Trust. Without trust, these new arrangements and new ways of working are destined to fail.

Let's go back 15 years, well before working from home was the norm. I had someone on my team who asked if they could work from home twice a week as the commute to the office was taking them two hours each way. I immediately agreed to this, as I trusted them … or so I thought. But I found myself, for some strange reason, checking in with them every few hours, asking how they were doing and if they needed my help. Even worse, this was before the days of Slack and Teams, so it was over the phone. After about two days of this, my employee finally said to me, "Do you not trust me?" I said, "Of course I do!" to which they responded, "Then why do you feel the need to check up on me every few hours?" I realized very quickly that my actions said loud and clear that I *didn't* trust them, and if I ever wanted to regain their trust I, not they, needed to start acting differently. And so I did!

Trust has been proven to help your people and business in a wide variety of ways. One study[42] found that employees in high-trust organizations are 50% more productive, 76% more engaged, have 74% lower stress levels, and have 40% less burnout than those in low-trust environments.

---

42   Paul J. Zak, Harvard Business Review, *The Neuroscience of Trust*, 2017.

This same study found that trust has a major impact on employee loyalty as well. Compared with employees at low-trust companies, 50% more of those working at high-trust organizations planned to stay with their company over the next year, and 88% more said they would recommend their company to family and friends as a place to work.

The cost of the trust tax

In Stephen M.R. Covey's book *Speed of Trust*, he talks about how trust affects two measurable outcomes – speed and cost. When trust goes down, speed decreases with it, with everything taking longer to do. Simultaneously, costs increase as there are redundancies in processes, with everyone checking up on everyone else, thus costing more. Covey calls this a tax, a "low-trust tax" where literally everything is being taxed because everything takes longer and costs more.

On the flip side, when trust is high, speed increases, and with it cost comes down. Everything happens faster and everything costs less because trust is flourishing. As Covey says, "That's a dividend, a high-trust dividend. It's really that simple, that real, that predictable."

As I read this it reminded me of the few times when I had not trusted one of my employees. I can remember double and triple-checking everything they did since I didn't trust their work. Thinking back, we both were paying the low-trust tax, slowing us down and costing us more time, which stemmed from a lack of trust.

ACTIONS TO TAKE

As we said with Respect, the good news about Trust is that as you get stronger with the other building blocks it will help you gain greater trust. But as with Respect, Trust also does not come automatically, it must be earned, which isn't easy. As Sinek says in his book *The Infinite*

Game, **"Trust is a feeling. Just as it is impossible for a leader to demand that we are happy or inspired, a leader cannot order us to trust them or each other."**

We've pulled together common themes from some fantastic books about trust, as well as our own learnings over the years when we've gotten it right (and wrong!) when it comes to trust.

Before we share these actions, let us make five key points about trust:

1. **The foundation is laid with respect** – We've said a few times how trust begins with respect, or how I often explain it – *respect opens the door to your people and trust lets them in.* For this reason, if you want to build trust, you need to start by building respect as a foundation. The previous Respect section can help you open this door with specific actions.

2. **It begins by trusting others** – As we said with respect, in order to earn trust you need to trust others. As Jim Kouzes and Barry Posner said in *The Five Practices of Exemplary Leadership,* "When it comes to building trust, leaders go first." And that's because there is no way that your people will trust you if you don't first begin by trusting them. Like respect, if you don't trust your people, start by understanding why. And remind yourself that you hired them because you thought they were the best candidate, right? So challenge yourself as to what may have changed to make you lose that trust.

3. **Trust is a process** – When I asked John Blakey, author of *The Trusted Executive,* what he thought one of the biggest mistakes that bosses make when it comes to trust, he said that it is thinking that trust involves only one thing, one action. If I keep my promises, I will be trusted, if I deliver on time, I will be trusted. If only it was that easy! As you'll see below, there are many dimensions, and many actions, that you need

to take to have a high-trust relationship with your people. It is a process and it takes time to build, depending and relying on many elements that ideally work together like a well-oiled machine.

4. **Trust is fragile** – As with respect, trust is absolutely fragile. It can take years to build, and moments to shatter and obliterate it. Or put another way, **trust is something that we earn by the teaspoon and lose by the barrel.**[43] You need to be vigilant in your efforts to strengthen and maintain trust on a continual basis.

5. **The opposite of trust is not distrust, it is control** – Many people think distrust or mistrust is the opposite of trust. That is actually not true, as the opposite of trust is control. Trust requires risk, namely the risk of giving up a degree of control. If you refuse to accept the risk of letting go and trusting someone, you're then forced to control them. Going back to our bad bosses, this is exactly how a Micromanager acts, not sharing information, or performing all the work themselves. And why do they do that? Because they don't trust anyone else to do it.

Show your people you genuinely care

Have you ever had a selfish boss, one that cares for themselves more than their team? Even if an action looks good on the surface, you know it's really for them, not you. Well I have, and in these cases, there is no way in hell that I would ever trust them. Would you?

Caring for your people is paramount in building and maintaining a trusting relationship. And in a world that has become less trusting, the

---

43   Exploring your Mind, *Respect is Demanded, But Trust is Earned*, 2017.

standards and expectations have only increased. Being nice, being kind, and being reliable is a good start, but it's not enough. Care is no longer a nice thing to do, but an integral part in building and maintaining trust and employee engagement. Here are a few ways to build trust by showing care:

Give a damn

In Scott's book *Radical Candor*, she talks about giving a damn when she describes how you care for your people, or as she defines it, "caring personally." Scott goes on to say that it's about caring about their needs and priorities, showing them not just your work self. We thought we'd borrow this to point out how critical it is when it comes to trust. Giving a damn and showing your people that you value them is where trust begins and ends. This happens by bringing out building blocks such as Empathy, Compassion, and Vulnerability, which individually and collectively show your people that you care about them.

Earlier in my career I thought that I was too busy for these "give a damn" actions. My job as a boss was to get work done, and that's what I focused on rather than building relationships. This was the way, until I turned in my two-week notice before moving to another company. I relaxed a bit more, paused to spend more time with my people, showed them my true self, and supported them in more empathetic and compassionate ways. And as I left they surprised me by saying that they wished I had acted this way earlier and that it would have completely changed their relationship with me, leading to more respect and trust from them. Lesson learned, and from that job onwards, you can be sure I've "given a damn" for my people.

Focus on psychological safety

Another key element of care and trust is psychological safety. Professor Amy Edmondson of Harvard Business School defines it as a "shared belief held by members of a team that it's okay to take risks, to express ideas and concerns, to speak up with questions, and to admit mistakes – all without fear of negative consequences." Studies have shown that creating an environment of psychological safety can deliver excellent results. One study[44] conducted by Edmondson reported higher productivity (50%), higher employee engagement (76%), less stress (74%), higher life satisfaction (29%) and a reduction in turnover (27%). These are obviously all great things, but what does this have to do with trust?

Well, everything. And that's because trust will not and cannot develop and flourish if your people don't feel safe. If I think back to what caused the most problems when I was working for my own original "bad boss," a lot of it had to do with a lack of psychological safety. Everything they did made me feel unsafe, vulnerable, and certainly not cared for. And, of course, there was absolutely no trust between us.

Support growth

Another way to make your people feel cared for is by supporting their growth. What you do (and don't do) to help them learn, develop, and grow speaks volumes about how much you care about them, and in return how much they can trust you. Because, as the famous saying from *Dirty Dancing* says, someone who trusts you would never want to "put baby in the corner" and force you to sit out on something important to you. If your people are going to trust you they need to see you helping them get out of the corner to learn, develop, and grow. We cover this in more depth in the Development and Coaching building blocks later on in this book.

Have your people's back

And finally, if you want your people to trust you, you need to have their back. They need to see you fighting for them, even when the going gets tough, and it's risky to do so. This can help build even more psychological safety at work.

---

44   Accenture and Amy Edmondson, *The Fearless Organization*, 2021.

I'm reminded of a very heated leadership team meeting, where I was presenting an opinion that was very different from everyone else. As colleagues interrupted me one by one to challenge me, trying to convince me to change my opinion, my boss jumped in and told everyone to hear me out. In that moment, I felt safe and cared for, and my trust in him increased even more. Very different from how another boss treated me, where my opinion was once again met with interruptions and rudeness. But this time, my boss didn't jump in to help me, and let everyone else bully me into accepting their beliefs. The result isn't surprising. I felt dejected and uncared for, and although I did trust this boss, they lost a few points of credit from the trust bank.

Do the right thing

We've illustrated that it's hard to trust someone if they don't show care. But what about integrity? Would you trust someone who you feel didn't do the "right thing"? Someone who doesn't act with integrity, honesty, and transparency? As one of my previous bosses explained to me, your job as a boss is not to make the popular decisions, it's to make the right decisions. And that's exactly what we need to do to fulfill our job as a boss, but also in order to build and maintain trust. In this section, we'll explore more ways to do just that.

Be open, honest and transparent

In *The Trusted Executive*, John Blakey says that we need to "choose to be open," citing a study[45] finding that openness is by far the single most important driver of trust. He explains that being open involves "speaking the truth and then giving something more." I like to describe the "something more" as sharing the entire story – beginning, middle, and end. Without this, your people fill in the blanks themselves and lose trust in you for not doing so yourself, or, worse,

---

45   Institute of Leadership and Management survey, 2014.

they may think you're hiding things from them and this again depletes your "trust bank." There are nuances and dangers in oversharing, but this is further covered in the Communication building block section.

Be consistently authentic

Another way to be open and honest is to be authentic. As we described in the Authenticity building block, it's about aligning your actions and behaviors in a way that is true to who you are (your true self) and what you believe in (your values). Doing the right thing means doing it on a continuous and consistent basis. You can't cherry-pick when you're going to do the right thing and when you're not, when it's convenient, and when it's either too much effort or too difficult. When you give your word, keep it. If you commit to something, follow through. If you agree to something, do what you promised. Keep to your authentic self, and to your word. It's as simple as that! Or as former U.S. President John F. Kennedy once said, "I would rather be accused of breaking precedents than breaking promises."

> **"Every leader needs to ask a very important, look-in-the-mirror question: Does my behavior increase trust? If you are considering elevating your leadership skills, trust is a pillar your leadership should stand on. It's the kind of trust that is developed when leaders confront reality, talk straight, display authenticity, and practice accountability." — *Marcel Schwantes, Global speaker, author, and leadership coach***

Zip it

This next action may come as a surprise, but it involves another element of doing the right thing. It comes from stories that people shared with us about bad bosses they've had, ones that we would have called Blabbers. Though they're not in our original top 10 bad bosses, we decided instead to include them here, in our Trust building block. One of the things that can completely destroy all of the great work that you've done to build trust is the case of the blabbers, where a boss shares information that has been confidentially told to them by an employee. **The absolute only reason to blab is to protect someone.** So, to maintain trust, it's really easy. As the title of this action says, zip it! Keep it confidential between you and that person.

Equally, if not even more important when deciding to zip it is privacy. It's something that as a boss we need to respect and protect. It seems obvious, but then you hear of a story that was shared with us, involving a boss who invaded their employee's privacy by logging into their computer and sending an email that the colleague didn't write. The email was to her boyfriend to cancel their plans because the employee had said no to attending a last-minute business function and the boss wanted them to go. Needless to say, this person didn't last long with their boss and their company, and a lack of trust had a lot to do with it.

Be a goldfish

This next action focuses on how *you maintain trust with your people*. If you trust your people, that's great, but how do you maintain this and ensure this trust is kept with you and your people? As a boss, this is a critical role for you to play.

Trust may be fragile. But as a boss, you can give your people the opportunity and the space to be trusted, letting them prove themselves to you and not flipping your trust switch on and off at every mistake. The best way to explain this is using the *Ted Lasso* phrase "be a goldfish," which Coach Lasso says to his star defender, Sam Obisanya. Lasso explained that a goldfish only has a 10-second memory, stressing the point that you need to move on from mistakes rather than lingering on them. This is such a powerful phrase in life, and especially when it comes to trust, for too often I've seen bosses lose trust in their people because of one small mistake or error in judgment that they may have made. Just like our people have trust credit for us, we need to do the same with them, moving on quickly, and giving them the chance to build back the trust credit. And by role modeling this with them, they will do the same with you. So, it's a win-win.

NEXT STEPS

☐ Think back to a time when trust broke down in a work relationship for you. What could you have done differently to prevent this from happening? Could you have used any of the tips or actions in this section to prevent this?

☐ Assess what you are doing now to create psychological safety, and what you can do in the future to improve it.

☐ Discuss with your people what trust means to them. How do you expect to earn trust, and how is it maintained, on a free-flowing basis?

☐ What can you do going forward to ensure that your people trust that you'll do the right thing?

LISTENING

Key Building Block for the Ignorer and the Coercer

As children we are taught to listen, that we should listen to our parents and teachers as a way to show them respect and to learn from them. When we enter the workplace, we again are told to listen for these same reasons. But instead of teachers or parents, listening continues to be "assigned" in an upward direction to listen to those more senior to us. And then we become a boss, and we're told that in addition to listening upward we now *also* need to listen downward, which means listening to our people.

But as shared earlier in the book, unfortunately, many bosses get this wrong. The survey we conducted for this book found that almost **eight out of 10 people have had a boss who doesn't listen to them** (an Ignorer boss), And another survey[46] found that **six out of 10 people believe their views and opinions are ignored**.

Quite frankly, this data doesn't surprise me. And that's because by changing the direction of our listening to be both up and down, we must drastically change our listening process and actions. I like to describe it as going from doing a forward somersault, which feels easy and natural, to doing a backward somersault, which is much harder to master. (Don't believe me? Go ahead, try it!)

To add to the need to master both directions of listening, the past few years has given us even *more* challenges. With more of our people working remotely and having to lead an increasingly diverse team, it means we have more obstacles and roadblocks to overcome when

---

46   The Workforce Institute, *The Heard and the Heard-Nots* report, 2021.

it comes to how to get listening right. So going back to my backward somersault analogy, now add to *that* having to do one on an incline. Tough, right?

WHY IT MATTERS

But with this difficulty comes rewards, for there are many ways that Listening can help you and your business. For example, it can help you build trust and solid relationships with your people as it shows them that you respect and care about them. It can drive collaboration and innovation as it encourages your people to work together and contribute their ideas. And it can create a greater sense of belonging as your people feel that their voice is heard and that they're a part of your team and the company.

Listening is a practice of being generous. Without saying a word, you can send the message to your people that what they are saying to you is important, that you value their input, and that you care and respect them enough to listen to them.

Here are three other reasons from The Workforce Institute's study[47] which explain why getting listening right is so important:

1. **Employees are more engaged** – 74% of employees feel more engaged at work, are more satisfied and motivated, when they think their voice is heard.

2. **Employees are more effective** – 74% of employees are more effective, so performing at a higher level, when they think their voice is heard.

---

47   The Workforce Institute, *The Heard and the Heard-Nots* report, 2021.

3. **Companies are more profitable** – 88% of employees whose companies financially outperform their competitors feel heard versus only 62% of employees at financially underperforming companies.

ACTIONS TO TAKE

Being a great listener doesn't always come easy, and sometimes it doesn't even feel very natural. But there are some things you can put into practice to help you be a better listener, which we'll now share.

Sometimes you need to shut up and listen

I know it's obvious, that when you're listening to others you should, well, listen. But how often do you forget about this and find yourself caught up in the moment, eagerly wanting to interrupt with something to say or ask? It's only natural, but let me ask you, have you ever thought of the impact this has on your people? How it makes them feel, and how it may prevent them from sharing in the future? This also impacts what you receive, as you may miss out on important thoughts and ideas, or misunderstand what was being communicated.

> **"We have two ears and one tongue so that we would listen more and talk less,"** *Diogenes*

You may be wondering why I titled this "shut up and listen." It's because in my book *Build it: The Rebel Playbook for Employee Engagement*, I share the story of HSBC bank's "Shut Up and Listen Program." It is a forum they created to help employees share their thoughts and views freely, creating an environment where employees felt they could not only speak up, but feel that it was their responsibility to do so. There are three rules for these meetings – the manager does not talk but just listens (thus the name of the program), there is no agenda, and the time belongs to the employees. At the start, it was a bit challenging, with many managers finding the art of being quiet uncomfortable and confusing, but then managers quickly realized the value of this approach and the results it helped them achieve. By the way, since sharing this story in the book and in talks, many companies and bosses have adopted this unique and effective approach. Give it a try!

The poker chip approach

In Liz Wiseman's book *Multipliers* she shares another approach for helping you listen more and dominate less in discussions, which she calls the "poker chip approach." You give yourself a certain number of poker chips, each color worth a number of seconds of talk time (e.g. one color is worth 120 seconds, another 90 seconds, and another 30 seconds). Each time you want to contribute in the meeting you need to "spend" the poker chip, which helps you exercise restraint, filtering which thoughts are poker chip-worthy.

Wiseman explains her client's reaction to this process where he was given five chips, "After the initial shock and bemusement (wondering how he could possibly convey all his ideas in five comments), he accepted the challenge. I watched as he carefully restrained himself, filtering his thoughts for only the most essential and looking for the right moment to insert his ideas."

Encourage speaking up

Another obvious point to make is that you can't listen if your people aren't saying anything. That's why it's absolutely critical for you to **create an environment where it's safe to speak up**, and encourage your people to do so. At a previous company, one of our company values was "Speak Up." I loved this value as it encouraged our people to speak their minds, creating a culture where they felt empowered to use their voice.

Here's how we described the Speak Up value to our people: "We discuss, debate, share views, listen, and develop our position. We are confident but never bullish. Our passion for the best outcome means that we don't always agree but we respect diversity, differences, and decisions made after debate."

Here are four things you can do to encourage and empower your people to speak up and use their voice:

1. **Let everyone know they have a voice –** In an article[48] by Timothy R. Clark he says, "Inclusion is the key that unlocks a team's cognitive diversity, but that inclusion must be built on a basic acceptance of any individual's worth – not their worthiness, which implies a performance test to meet a standard or requirement of some kind."

   If you want your employees to feel confident to speak up, they must first feel this sense of acceptance, making it clear that everyone's voice matters, regardless of their seniority, etc. I saw this happen time and time again at my company with the Speak Up value, as people of all job levels and seniority freely jumped into discussions, and each was given the floor and the respect they deserved. And I have to say it was amazing!

---

48   Timothy R. Clark, Harvard Business Review, *Building a Culture Where Employees Feel Free to Speak Up*, 2023.

Inclusive approach to listening

Unfortunately many companies are not practicing an inclusive approach to listening. One study[49] found that almost half (47%) of employees say that **underrepresented voices aren't being heard**. And from an age perspective, this same study found that just 16% of Gen Z workers feel they can freely express their views and opinions with their manager, compared to 67% of their older colleagues. Ask yourself, who *aren't* you hearing from, and why?

---

2. **Don't give lip service –** An inclusive approach doesn't just involve who you listen to, but *when* you listen to them. One of the things that will really piss your people off is listening to them too late, once decisions have already been determined and made. I call things like this a "why bother," as all you're doing is paying lip service to your people by pretending that you want to listen to them. In reality, if you did care, you would have come to them sooner. So now, you're wasting your time and theirs. What's more, you're negatively impacting their trust and engagement with a fake "listen," at a time when it doesn't matter, as the decision has been made. Going back to speaking up, you can guarantee next time they won't!

3. **Give your people permission to disagree –** Speaking up should not just happen in one way, your way, with your people agreeing with what you have to say, or sharing ideas that they think will please or impress you. That completely takes away from the richness of their contributions and undermines your team's ability to be innovative and effective.

   As Clark says, "When loyalty becomes contingent on agreement, it produces manipulated conformity, which isn't loyalty at all. Unless the organization divorces loyalty from

---

49   The Workforce Institute, *The Heard and the Heard-Nots* report, 2021.

agreement, the pressure to conform can produce dangerous groupthink."

4. **Separate permission from adoption** – And finally, a common misconception is that when your people speak up and share their suggestions and ideas it means that you have to say yes to each and every one of them. It can feel overwhelming, so bosses will put hurdles in place so that their people do not speak up. But in reality, just because your person has put forward an idea, you have no obligation to say yes, to adopt or move forward with it.

You do, however, need to make it a point to acknowledge and commend those who speak up, even when you won't be adopting their suggestion. As Clark says, "To speak up, an employee needs some evidence of organizational receptivity. Is someone listening? Does it even matter? Will it make a difference? In the absence of adoption, emphasize recognition. We all need the reassurance that when the answer is no, the very act of speaking up is appreciated and encouraged."

Read between the lines

A helpful concept I've learned over the years is that of reading between the lines, which involves looking past the words your people are saying as you listen to them in order to understand the deeper and true meaning. The Japanese have a different way of putting it, using the words "kuuki yomeru," which literally means "reading the air." I really like this as I can just picture words popping up to show me what a person is truly thinking while others are listening to them. To help you with this, here are two things to think about:

1. **Dig deep** – First, it's important to dig deep, not just accepting what's said on the surface, but digging deeper to understand

more. What is the root cause or message of what your people are trying to say? A great technique for this was developed by Toyota Sakichi Toyoda, and is called "The 5 Whys." As the title suggests, you ask the question "why?" five times, or until you get to the root cause, thus digging below the surface.

To bring this to life, let's say your employee comes to you with a suggestion to change from having daily 15-minute team calls to an hour-long call on a Friday morning. You could just agree to it, or you could do this exercise to help you read between the lines and get to a deeper understanding, which in this case is that the problem isn't the calls but the reporting system.

You Say	They Say
Why do you want to make this change?	Because I don't feel it's a good use of our time talking every morning.
Why isn't it a good use of your time?	Because we spend a lot of time not only being on the calls but preparing for them.
Why are you spending so much time preparing?	Because we have to look at multiple reports to pull together the data to report on.
Why do you need to look at multiple reports?	Because there isn't one report that has all of the information we need to share.
Would it be a good idea for me to request a report be created so you only need to look at this one?	Yes, that would be perfect, thank you for this, let's keep the daily calls then.

2. **Look out for nonverbal cues** – Next, be on the lookout for nonverbal cues your people are sending you, both conscious and unconscious. Look for changes in their facial expressions (e.g. have they raised an eyebrow, changed the shape of their mouth?), eye contact (has it increased or decreased?), posture (e.g. are they leaning away from you, crossing their arms?), and even gestures (e.g. are they pointing a finger, clenching a fist?).

"Meaning isn't always found in the words themselves but rather in the spaces in between the lines." — *Michelle Sandlin, American writer*

Master the art of listening

As you work to be a better listener, an approach I've used for many years is something called "active listening," which was first coined by Carl Rogers and Richard Farson back in 1957. It takes listening from being one-dimensional, with words merely being said, to a multidimensional approach where words more freely flow, flourish, and achieve so much more. As said by Rogers, active listening "shows the speaker that we grasp, from his point of view, just what it is he is communicating to us. More than that, we convey to the speaker that we are seeing things from his point of view." By doing this, it shows your people that if they are going to take the time to talk to you, you are going to take the time and care to listen to them, and by doing so encourages openness, honesty, and a more trusting relationship.

"Active listening is the doorway to increased belonging, loyalty, profitability, innovation, and so much more. It is the difference between thinking we understand what people want and knowing what they want." — *Heather R. Younger, The Art of Active Listening*

There are many solid and effective methods and models that provide the steps of active listening. One model I'd like to share is called "The Cycle of Active Listening™," which comes from Heather R. Younger's book *The Art of Active Listening*. Here is a high-level summary of the five steps that drive a continuous, dynamic, and never-ending process of listening:

1. **Recognize the Unsaid** – The first step is to recognize the unsaid, which is something I referred to in the previous bullet when I talked about reading between the lines. This helps you pick up important signals and cues that your people are sending your way, helping you have a broader and deeper understanding so that you can then address it more effectively.

2. **Seek to Understand** – This next step, seek to understand, has been a mantra of mine ever since I read Covey's book titled *The 7 Habits of Highly Effective People*, where he listed his fifth habit as "Seek First To Understand, Then To Be Understood." For many, this is a paradigm or mindset shift as it involves stepping away and outside of your personal experiences to understand and uncover the perspectives of your people. As with the previous step, this helps us fully understand our people, giving them the chance and the floor to tell their full story.

   As Younger says, "When we go into interactions with little knowledge and the intent to seek the truth and learn, we automatically become more curious about what the other might teach us. Think about little kindergarten students in a classroom who are listening to a history lesson about an interesting character. Their eyes get big, and they are excited to find out what might come next. We need to enter our interactions wide-eyed and open to what we might find."

3. **Decode** – Next, we need to decode, which as someone who loves doing puzzles, always puts a smile on my face. It involves interpreting, reflecting or researching what you think you've heard your people say. It's about identifying if there are any gaps in what you've heard, and thus do you need to go back and ask any additional questions. And it's also connecting what you're hearing from your people, drawing meaning and connections from seemingly unrelated words. This step is important because if we jump into action without decoding, we often misunderstand and/or take the wrong action.

4. **Act** – Now that you've taken everything in and have decoded it, it's time to act. This is something that is often missed or forgotten, with one survey[50] finding that 40% of employees don't feel their feedback leads to actionable change. Not only does this help you drive action and change, but also because this step signals to your people that what they've just shared with you will not sit on a piece of paper, in a drawer, or in a file on your computer. It's here where you show your commitment to bringing their voices to life by taking the necessary and appropriate action.

5. **Close the Loop** – The final step is closing the loop, where the cycle of active listening is complete. It can be as simple as thanking someone for sharing their views, or something a bit comprehensive such as publishing a six-month action plan. But bottom line, it shows your people what you've done or will do with what you've shared with them.

---

50   The Workforce Institute, *The Heard and the Heard-Nots* report, 2021.

NEXT STEPS

☐ Think back to a time when you misunderstood what one of your people said to you. What caused this? What problems did it cause? What could you do differently the next time?

☐ Talk to your people to find out how well they'd say you listen to them. Are there things you are doing really well? Are there things you could do better?

☐ What two or three things can you do differently to improve your listening skills, taking on board the tips and actions shared in this section?

COMMUNICATION

Key Building Block for the Avoider, the Hoarder, and the Blamer

It should come as no surprise to see Communication as one of the building blocks, for as with Listening, it's how we "do things," how we work together with our people and with other teams. But what you may not have considered is that besides it being important on its own, it's also critical to so many of the other blocks. For example, if you don't communicate well you'll never be able to effectively show appreciation, provide feedback, coach others, and so on. And for this reason, although it's not listed as one of the foundational blocks, it does have a major role to play in supporting the other building blocks.

As with listening, unfortunately many bosses get communication wrong. In fact, the survey we conducted for this book found that more than **seven out of 10 (74%) of people have had a boss who doesn't communicate effectively to them** (a Hoarder boss). That's a lot!

I find this unsurprising though, because when it comes to communication, our role changes when we become a boss, and many take time to get used to it. Take basketball for example, to illustrate this point. Think about the difference between a player whose role it is to pass the ball compared to someone whose role it is to score baskets. The player throwing the ball doesn't need to be as precise and accurate because the person catching their throw can move to where the ball goes. On the other hand, the scorer (the boss in this scenario) needs to get the ball directly into the basket, so they need to make sure that their throw is spot-on in order to score. The same is true for you as a boss as you "throw" your communication to your people, making sure that it gets "in the basket" and that you score through communication.

"**Communications is not a soft skill, it is a rock hard competency, as important as any other skill**" — *Sally Susman, Breaking Through: Communicating to Open Minds, Move Hearts, and Change the World*

WHY IT MATTERS

When done well, Communication can have a profound impact on your people and on your business. It can boost employee morale and satisfaction, drive productivity, and improve trust, collaboration, and cooperation. Add these together, and they contribute to your company's success, and to your own personal success as a boss.

On the flip side, it can have negative consequences when it's not done well or when miscommunication occurs, and these mistakes add up to impact your company's bottom line. We shared some data on this when we covered the Hoarder boss, but here's another study[51] showing what the cost of **poor communication can lead to**:

- **Wasted time** – 68% of survey respondents

- **Missed messages** – 53% of survey respondents

- **Burnout, stress, and fatigue** – 42% of survey respondents

- **Bad customer experience** – 30% of survey respondents

- **Lost customers to competitors** – 12% of survey respondents

---

51   Project.co's, Communication Statistics report, 2023.

ACTIONS TO TAKE

If you find communicating with your employees challenging and daunting, you are not alone. In fact, one survey[52] found that **69% of managers admitted feeling uncomfortable communicating with their employees**, being uncomfortable with "becoming vulnerable, recognizing achievements, delivering the 'company line,' giving clear directions, crediting others with having good ideas, speaking face to face, and having difficult feedback conversations in general."

It doesn't surprise me that so many bosses find communication daunting. Unlike with basketball when the hoop is always the same, always 10 feet above the floor, our employees are far from being the same. That's because people take in and translate information in different ways when they receive communications. That constant pressure of "scoring" with what you're trying to communicate leads to worrying, and often, even an "air ball." But there are some things you can put into practice to help you be a better communicator, and here are some to get you started.

Communicate continuously

The key to being a great communicator is understanding that **once is never enough**. Going back to the basketball analogy, last time I promise, if your job is to score baskets, you don't just score one and then sit on the bench for the remainder of the game. You keep finding new ways to score and, ultimately, win. The same is true when it comes to communicating, as it needs to happen over and over again. With communication you should be using a wide variety of methods and channels to help you "score," to get your messages through to your people by sharing them at the *right time* and in the *right way*.

---

52   Interact, U.S. Survey, 2018.

Don't fall into the assumption trap, assuming your people already know things. Assume the worst and over-communicate, letting them decide when or if they should ignore something.

For example, let's take something simple like letting your team know that during the summer, your company has decided employees can leave on Fridays at noon. You may first tell them this during your weekly team call, but since not everyone attended and there was lots of information shared, you could then follow it up with an email. You might then send an email or a team message via Slack, Teams, etc. at the start of the first week this takes effect, listing out dates. Then you may want to do the same week before it ends so that no one gets it wrong.

Now this may seem like a lot of work, a bit of a slog repeating yourself over and over again, but doing it this way can help prevent misunderstandings and make sure everyone is on the same page to set them up for success. Think of it like a puzzle, if you aren't given all of the pieces of the puzzle you'll never finish it, and you'll never see the final image. The same is true with communication, for if your people don't receive information continuously they'll never be able to "complete the puzzle," having all of the "pieces" of information they need to do their job well.

How quickly we forget

According to the Ebbinghaus Forgetting Curve, we forget 50% of the information we receive within 30 minutes, between 70% to 80% after 24 hours, and up to 90% after seven days. This means that communicating continuously is even more necessary as we'll forget almost everything by the end of the week anyway.

Stop hiding behind the curtain

The *how* is just as important as the *when* in communicating. As a boss, you must get out from behind the curtain and communicate with your people in an open, honest, and transparent way. Without this, you risk your people not fully understanding and/or buying into the information, creating mistrust and disengagement, and fueling fear and uncertainty. From my experience, this can be just as detrimental as not sharing the information in the first place!

Your people deserve to hear the truth. And if you withhold it, they'll create their own version of the truth ... which is often worse than the actual truth!

Here are some things to help you get out from behind the curtain:

- The first is to **default to transparency**. Too often when we communicate to our people we automatically jump to the conclusion that we need to withhold information, believing there's no way that you can share all of it. It's time to flip this on its head, and instead start with the mindset of sharing *everything*, defaulting to transparency, and then only withholding something if you have a really good reason for doing so (e.g. it could negatively impact the business or an individual). This more transparent approach helps you more effectively communicate the information to your people and not keep them in the dark about trivial things.

- Next, when communicating with your people, remember **not to dress up the truth**. If you have something bad to share, just say it. Don't make it sound all sunshine and roses when it isn't. Your people deserve the truth, they need the truth, even when it's shitty truth!

"Lying to our staff, telling half-truths, withholding information and compulsive under-communication destroys trust in organizations. It creates an 'us and them' culture and sabotages any possibility of employee engagement. If you're serious about employee engagement, you need to stop the lies and build trust instead." — *Glenn Elliott and Debra Corey, Build it: The Rebel Playbook to Employee Engagement*

- Another key aspect of being transparent is **sharing and explaining the "why."** So not just the message and information, but *why you're sharing it* and *why it should matter* to them. This helps you complete the "puzzle" as we talked about before, but also brings your people into the coveted circle of trust, letting them know that you trust and respect them enough to be open and transparent with them.

  Let's go back to the previous example to illustrate this, the one where you've told your people they only work half days on Fridays during the summer months. The "why" is that your company is committed to supporting the wellbeing of your people, so in the summer, you're doing this by letting them enjoy the good weather and the time with their family and friends, without having to take additional days off. If you don't share this "why" with them, a few things could happen. First, they may not appreciate the positive and kind gesture that it is. And second, they may wonder why it's only happening in the summer and possibly be upset that it isn't continuing.

- And finally, it's important to **make room for questions and dissent**. Think of it this way, if a door is open, people can go both in and out of it, right? Well, the same is true when it comes to communications in that it needs to go both ways

– you communicating out to your people, and your people being able to communicate back to you. Whether that's with questions or to voice a differing opinion, you need to open the door to these possibilities. Without it, you risk losing the impact of openness and transparency, as your people will believe that you're hiding something. So let them ask you questions, even the hard ones, as it's better to address them in the moment than have them pile up and go unanswered.

Communicate with empathy

Another aspect of communication has to do with *the way* you communicate, e.g. the tone, words, and approach that you use. This is critical to keep in mind, for even if you communicate in the most transparent way, without empathy or bringing compassion to the situation, then it will fall flat and not meet your objectives.

Empathetic communication is delivering information in a way that understands and addresses the feelings and needs of the recipient. If done well, it's a win-win, with you being able to effectively "throw" the message to the recipient, and them being able to "catch" it as they're in the right space and frame of mind to do so.

At its core, communicating with empathy is putting yourself in the shoes of the recipient. Sometimes it's easy, as you may have been in their situation before, but if you haven't, this can be challenging. Regardless, it's critical to gain this perspective and understanding, and then use this to deliver information in an empathetic way based on what's right for them.

To help you with this, let's look at how to use empathy in what, when, and where you communicate information:

- **What** – Using empathy in sharing information is impacted by both *what information you share* and *what words you use*. Here's an example of when I got it wrong when it came to the first part …

  I had an employee who was on maternity leave, something I had never been on myself at this point in time. Because of this, I couldn't put myself in her shoes and didn't do what I now understand to be important, which was to ask her what kind of information she wanted from me during this period of time. The result was that I hoarded information, not sharing it with her because I thought she wouldn't want it, thinking that she'd be too busy taking care of her newborn to read any of it. Wrong! When she came back from her leave she was quite angry with me for doing this, saying that the information would have helped her feel more connected to the business and her colleagues, and would have made her transition back to work much easier. Ouch, did I get this wrong or what?

- **When** – Believe it or not, the *timing* of when you share information can have an impact on how it makes your people feel, and thus needs to be addressed in an empathetic way. Here's an example from our friend Pat, with a boss who got it completely wrong.

The situation was that on Pat's last working day before they had a week off for the holiday season, Pat's boss said that they needed to talk to them immediately. They jumped on a call, where Pat was told that the team was going to be reorganized and that Pat would find out more detail when they came back from the holiday break. As you can imagine, Pat panicked, wondering how this would impact them and their team, and spent the entire week worrying about it instead of enjoying the holiday with their family and friends. In this situation my challenge to Pat's boss would have been, did you really need to do it then? What would have happened if you had waited another week?

- **Where** – Another thing you may not have considered is where you share and put the information. Do you share it in an email, on a team call, or even a text? There are so many ways to do it, so think about what will work best for your people and for the specific communication.

  You also may want to signpost your people to find out more information on their own, especially if it's something that is ongoing or far into the future. What kind of FAQ or other information do your employees need, to save you time from answering questions, but also so they feel the most informed?

Don't assume they understand

The final thing to consider and to close out your communication loop, is the concept of checking for understanding. Time and time again I've seen bosses communicate to their people and just walk away, assuming that their job is done. Well, it ain't! The loop is not closed until you are absolutely sure that your people understand the intent and meaning of your communication. Remember that we all interpret things differently, so what goes in (what you say) is not always what goes out (what your people understand).

To make this point, when I run workshops I play a popular childhood game, in some countries called "Telephone," or "Whisper Down the Lane." The way it works is that I break the group out into smaller groups, and then one by one whisper the same message into the ear of the first person in each group. They then whisper the message from one person to another until the final person shares back to everyone what has been said. The results are quite amusing as the message typically gets changed a lot throughout the process. Point made, and hopefully, these bosses keep this in mind next time they communicate with their people!

NEXT STEPS

☐ Think back to a time when you communicated and it didn't go well. What went wrong? What lessons did you learn? What could you have done differently?

☐ Now think back to a time when your communication rocked, when your people came up to you afterwards and thanked you for being so open and honest with them. What did you do differently that landed well, and what can you do in the future to replicate this result?

☐ Talk to your people about their communication preferences. Ask how they like to be communicated to, when, and any other pieces of feedback they can share with you to improve how you communicate with them.

☐ What two or three things can you do differently to improve your communication, taking on board the tips and actions shared in this section?

FEEDBACK

Key Building Block for the Avoider, the Pretender, and the Blamer

Let me ask you a question. When I say the word "feedback" do you get a sick feeling in the pit of your stomach? Well, you're not alone, for every time I teach a course on feedback almost every person in the class, regardless of job level or years as a boss, says that they dread giving feedback, even when it's positive feedback. When asked why, the most common responses are the *fear of the unknown*. How will the recipient handle the feedback? Will they get upset, defensive, or even burst into tears? Or, some bosses have a *fear of the consequences*. What will this do to my relationship with this person and to my credibility?

And while this is all normal (for me, too!), I urge you to not let this stop you from giving the feedback that your people need. We covered some of this when we spoke about the Avoider boss, but since this is the second most common type of boss (80% of people surveyed said they've had one), let's go into a little more detail.

The truth is, without feedback, it's as though your people are on a sailboat without a rudder. If you've never sailed before, the rudder is what you use to steer the boat, helping you change direction and stay on course. Without it, your people end up going wherever the wind takes them, which can be in conflict with how you're trying to achieve team goals.

And now, let's go on to a story from Pat, as told to me during one of my feedback classes …

One day Pat went into work with toothpaste on their face as they'd been in such a rush in the morning that they hadn't looked in the mirror. Pat went from meeting to meeting, and not until their last meeting of the day did someone actually tell them about the toothpaste on their face. Everyone must have thought, I don't want to tell Pat, someone else will. Or, I can't tell them as they'll be so embarrassed. I love this story because every time I doubt whether I should give feedback, I ask myself, "Do I want this person to walk around with toothpaste on their face all day or should I take responsibility and give them the feedback?"

WHY IT MATTERS

We've just shared a few reasons why feedback matters, but let's add to this with more reasons and data:

1. **Your people want more feedback –** The first piece of data says that 65%[53] of people don't just want feedback, but they want *more* feedback.

2. **Your people want it frequently –** The second piece of data says that 60%[54] of people *want feedback on a daily or weekly basis.*

3. **Your people want negative feedback –** Next, one study showed that 92% of people surveyed, so almost everyone, said they'd want to receive even negative feedback if it was delivered appropriately, as they felt it would improve their performance.

4. **Your people are more motivated –** And finally, data shows that companies that practice effective feedback have employees who are 3.6 times more likely to strongly agree that it motivates them to do outstanding work.

---

53   OfficeVibe study, 2017.
54   PwC study, 2018.

This makes it really clear – you can't ignore giving feedback any longer!

ACTIONS TO TAKE

And while you may never be 100% comfortable giving feedback (the truth can hurt, I know), you can take action to get better at it. Here are some ideas to get started:

Remove the emotion

When it comes to giving feedback, it's key to leave the emotions at the door, and not let them enter your conversation. They have no place in a feedback discussion. Why? Because you have a job to deliver a message, and that should be the focus of what you are trying to do. If I think back to feedback disasters, emotion was definitely in the room, disturbing and derailing things, moving it from a conversation to a heated debate or argument. To avoid this, you need to keep the conversation constructive and detached from emotion instead of making it personal and confrontational.

A model I often share that gives you the focus and structure to do this is called the FAST feedback model. **Frequent** (given when your people need it), **Accurate** (not hearsay or stuff dug up from the past), **Specific** (give concrete examples), **and Timely** (delivered as close to the situation as possible). So when you give feedback, remember to make it FAST!

Go in prepared

Next, let me ask you a question, do you ever go to the supermarket hungry? We all do this from time to time, and the result is that you end up buying impulse food, not what you really need (picture bags of cookies, salty snacks, and expensive chocolate instead of or in addition to the milk, butter, fruit and veggies that are on your list). Well, the same is true when it comes to giving feedback. If you go into your feedback session with your employee "hungry," as in, not prepared, it won't end well. In fact, if I again think back on my feedback disasters, to some extent they all had some element of lack of planning that made it end up this way.

Here are three things to consider as you prepare to give feedback:

1. **Remove barriers –** The first thing to do is to remove barriers, both physical and mental barriers. A great way to think of this comes from Brown's book *Daring Greatly*, where she explains it as saying to yourself "I'm prepared to put the problem in front of us rather than between us."

   Removing barriers can mean a number of different things. For example, can you sit next to the person instead of with a desk between you? Can you start out the conversation with an understanding that it's a shared problem, something you'll sort out together and not try to point fingers or force blame, to avoid defensive barriers? Whatever you do, figure out what the barriers may be beforehand, and plan out how you'll remove or overcome them so that they don't trip up the conversation and prevent you from meeting your feedback objectives.

2. **Get ready to listen –** The next thing to do is to prepare and get ready to listen. Now I know this seems pretty obvious, but often what happens in feedback situations is that you go in committed to sharing your story and your point of view, and you get so caught up in it that you don't give the other person the time and space to do the same. If instead, you go in ready to listen, to ask questions, to understand their perspective and their "why," you'll end up in a much better place. Remind yourself that **feedback is a conversation, not a sermon.**

3. **Scenario plan –** The final thing to do is to think through different scenarios, which I call the mapping exercise. I like to map out all of the things I can possibly imagine the other person saying or raising, and then map out how I'll respond and handle each of them. This helps me feel more confident in these challenging situations but also allows me to think through how things will play out during the feedback conversation. However, it's equally important to be open-minded and flexible if and when things *don't* go to plan, and not let that throw you off. Going back to the sailboat analogy, have your route mapped out, but be flexible and adapt should you encounter storms and challenges that may come your way.

Give a gift and not punishment

Another common mistake when it comes to feedback is giving it in the wrong way. You might get caught up in the moment, in the emotions, or in the surprises your employee is throwing your way, and the feedback ends up being delivered as a punishment and not the gift as it was intended.

I've read tons of books on feedback, and the one that completely changed how I think about and give feedback is *Radical Candor* by Scott. In it, Scott shares her simple yet effective feedback model that, as she explains, helps you "be a great boss without losing your humility." Perfect!

I'll leave it to Scott to explain the details in her book, but to give you an overview of it, her model has two axes. The first one is the "care personally" axis, or what Scott calls the "give a damn" axis, which we briefly discussed in our Trust building block. It's where we show human kindness and compassion to one another, caring about each other in how we give feedback.

The second axis is the "challenge directly" axis, or what Scott calls the "willing to piss people off" axis. This is where we need to forget what our parents and teachers told us when they said "If you don't have anything nice to say, don't say anything at all," because this doesn't work in feedback, as it's our responsibility and obligation to say the truth and to challenge directly.

She shares the following four feedback styles within the axes:

1. **Ruinous empathy –** This is where most people are when it comes to feedback, and is when you care too much but fail to challenge directly. We do this because we want to spare someone's feelings, so we sugar-coat what we say, don't tell the whole truth, or often don't say anything at all. This is often done by the Avoider and Pretender bosses, and is ultimately unhelpful and often can be damaging to you and the person who needs the feedback.

2. **Manipulative insincerity –** This is when you fail in both axes, so you're not caring and you're not effectively challenging. This is often described as backstabbing someone or being passive-aggressive, when you are insincere to the person's face, and then behind their back you criticize them. This is often done by the Blamer boss as a way to protect yourself, caring more about your own feelings and situation than the other person's.

3. **Obnoxious aggression –** This is where you challenge directly, but don't care personally. This is often described as front-stabbing or being brutally honest, and it's when you deliver feedback in an unkind way.

4. **Radical candor –** This is where you care personally and challenge directly. This is nirvana, the style we all need to aim for, with the feedback being given through a perfect balance of being both kind and clear, and specific and sincere.

Stay clear of the sandwich

You may have heard of the "sandwich approach" when it comes to feedback, when you deliver negative feedback sandwiched between two "slices" of positive feedback. And while it may feel easier, as the difficult part of giving feedback is sandwiched between the easy part, we believe that this carbohydrate-heavy method **just doesn't work**. It's not fair to your people (remember Scott's "give a damn" axis), it's not effective (remember Scott's "challenge directly" axis), and … your people know exactly what you're doing, which means the "bread" (positive feedback) just delivers empty "calories" and empty feedback. This doesn't mean your feedback needs to be all or nothing, all positive or all negative, because ultimately you want to deliver constructive feedback to help the person understand and develop. But just be careful how you position and blend it together. Maybe serve feedback as a salad instead of a sandwich?!

Bosses need feedback, too

So far we've been talking about you giving feedback to your people, but we couldn't close out this topic without mentioning the importance of feedback in the other direction – from your people to you. There are four key reasons why this is worth understanding. First, it gives you your people's thoughts and perspectives as to what you are doing well as their boss, and insight into areas where you can and should improve. Second, this brings additional insights into how they feel and what they need. For example, if they give you feedback saying they don't believe you value and appreciate them, even after you put them forward for a quarterly award, this tells you that this wasn't enough, wasn't the right kind of appreciation and/or that something else is missing which is causing them to feel this way. Third, it helps build trust with your people, as you're demonstrating your willingness to listen, learn, and change. And finally, by asking for feedback, it shows your people that you believe feedback is important, creating a feedback culture across your entire team. Win-win!

NEXT STEPS

☐ Think back to a time when you gave feedback to someone on your team and it didn't go well. What went wrong? What lessons did you learn? What could you have done differently?

☐ Now think back to a time when your feedback conversation went well, when you both left feeling like it was a constructive and helpful session. What did you do, and what can you take away from this to incorporate in future communications?

☐ Pick a real-life scenario where you have or will have to give feedback, and do a few role-play practice sessions to try out the approaches suggested in this section, making sure that you've prepared for the different reactions. Practice asking for honest feedback on this exercise and aim to improve each time.

APPRECIATION

Key Building Block for the Ignorer and the Unappreciater

The next building block follows on from the last, as Appreciation is a form of Feedback. It involves the simple act of showing your people that you recognize, acknowledge, and appreciate their efforts and accomplishments through positive feedback. At its core, it's about **looking for and seeing the "moments that matter"** by doing something constructive, meaningful, and personal to make your people **feel valued and appreciated for their contributions**.

But unfortunately of all of the bad boss types surveyed for this book, the one that doesn't give appreciation, the Unappreciater, was the most common. The survey showed that **over eight out of 10 (81%) people have had a boss who has not shown them appreciation**. And another survey[55] found that **65% of employees haven't received any form of recognition and appreciation for good work in the last year**. Forget the last quarter, month, or week, in an entire year not one boss, good or bad, has shown them appreciation … no wonder so many survey respondents said their boss was an Unappreciater!

I believe appreciation isn't happening for a few reasons. First, there are still too many bosses who don't understand the power and difference it can make to their people and the business. Second, though I've referred to appreciation as a "simple act," doing it right is actually far from simple! Yes, saying "thank you," isn't hard, but finding the right words and actions that will work for each of our very unique people can be difficult and daunting, similar to Feedback or Communication which varies from person to person. So some avoid it, sending a generic thank you message, or a meaningless gift. And, no surprise, their people don't feel appreciated!

---

55   Great Place to Work study, 2022.

"Sometimes managers wrongly see recognition as a 'tip,' believing that it doesn't need to be given as employees are already being paid to do their job. We need to challenge this so that everyone is valued for the work that they do. After all, if you don't provide recognition, your competitors will!" — *Judith Germain, Leadership Catalyst, The Maverick Paradox*

WHY IT MATTERS

The good news is that appreciation has statistically and scientifically been proven to motivate your people, improve their performance, drive business results and so much more. In fact, in my book written on appreciation titled *See it. Say it. Appreciate it!* I have an entire chapter devoted to what I call the "superpowers" of appreciation.

To give you a flavor of all what appreciation can do when it's done well, here are a few pieces of data from one report[56] showing that employees are:

- **Less likely to leave** – 5 times as likely to stay and grow at their organization.

- **More satisfied** – 44% more likely to be "thriving" in their life overall.

- **More productive** – 73% less likely to "always" or "very often" feel burned out.

---

56 Gallup, *Transforming Workplace Through Recognition*, 2023.

- **More engaged** – 4 times as likely to be actively engaged at work.

- **More connected** – 5 times as likely to feel connected to their workplace culture.

And since this book is for bosses, let me share two more pieces of data from another report[57] to highlight the impact that **appreciation from you** can have on your people:

- **Improved relationships** – 58% of employees report that their relationship with their boss would improve if they were given more recognition.

- **Improved trust** – Employees who were recognized were 34% more likely to trust their boss compared to those who had never been recognized.

There's also science behind the power of appreciation, with our brain releasing "happiness chemicals" when we are recognized and feel appreciated. These chemicals – dopamine, serotonin, and oxytocin, all influence how we feel, with sensations of happiness, closeness, and joy. And better yet, this chemical release "cements the knowledge that more of that behavior will create more praise, resulting in another chemical drench[58]."

> **"It's important to remember that everyone needs to be given good news, and to be thanked or recognized regularly." — Sue Kemp, Managing Director, Associated Independent Stores**

---

57   Achiever's, *State of Recognition* report, 2020.

58   Gallup, *In Praise of Praising Your People*, 2016.

ACTIONS TO TAKE

As mentioned earlier, giving and showing appreciation is not always easy. But there are some things you can put into practice to help you learn the art and science of showing appreciation. To help you with this, let me share with you from my book[59] what I call the "The Golden Rules of Appreciation," or the "Four Things You MUST Do." These are guiding philosophies and principles I've used and have shared with others over the years to help deliver genuine and meaningful appreciation to my people. Together, these four rules form the acronym MUST, creating a call to action, what we "must" do to deliver that appreciation feeling. Here is a high-level overview for each of these rules:

Rule 1 – Make appreciation meaningful

The letter "M" stands for **making appreciation meaningful** for your people. This is critical so that the recipient truly feels appreciated, and it happens when you deliver meaning in both *what you say* and *what you do*, showing your people that you have seen, value, and appreciate their specific contributions.

Your "say" is your appreciation messages, what you are actually saying/writing to your people. It can be easy to just say "thank you" and stop there, but if you attach a meaning to the words and explain the impact of what they've done, **the person knows specifically what they've done, and how they've helped you and others.** To help with this, whenever I run an appreciation training session, I share this simple three-step process that comes from Gregg Lederman's book, *Crave*:

---

59   Debra Corey, *See it. Say it. Appreciate it!*, 2022.

1. **Tell the Action** – Describe what the person did, their behavior or action, that is worthy of being recognized. Be specific about it so that they are absolutely clear on what they've done to earn your appreciation.

   Example: Thank you for jumping in to help me come up with the two new marketing campaign ideas that we can present to our client.

2. **Connect to a Value** – Next, link the behavior or action to your company values or specific focus area. Using your words, make it clear that what the person did has made a difference in achieving a priority or goal for you and the organization, with no second-guessing.

   Example: Your actions directly align with our company value of "create magic" as the new ideas are innovative and show the client a new way of thinking.

3. **Share the Impact** – Last, but certainly not least, use your message to show the benefit and impact of the behavior or action that you are recognizing. As Lederman says, "By sharing the impact, you are providing another healthy dose of respect and purpose!" Explain exactly what the impact was, why it matters, and how crucial and important their contributions have been. Connect their great work to the impact it has to elevate regular recognition to the kind of story that releases those happiness chemicals!

   Example: Your ideas and suggestions had a profound impact on the client selecting us to deliver their new marketing campaign and two more to follow. This would never have happened without your contributions. Thank you, you rock!

Just as important as the "say" is the "do," which creates a greater sense of appreciation through recognition rewards. These can either be non-financial, with just that message being the reward, or it can be financial, depending on the level of contribution. The key is not to just throw money, gifts or anything else at your people as a way to show appreciation without understanding more about the moment of recognition. Here arc two things to keep mind when selecting the right reward:

1. **What did they do?** – Consider the connection between the reward and the contribution, making sure that they're aligned. A smaller contribution might spark a small reward like a $5 coffee card, whereas a larger one might be a gift card to a favorite restaurant.

2. **What do they prefer?** – Consider differences in your workforce when determining rewards to meet their diverse set of needs. For example, at one of my previous companies, when we gave out a reward for someone who went above and beyond, we would give them a choice between a bottle of wine or nice chocolates. The reason we did this was that we understood not everyone drank or wanted to receive alcohol (or weren't old enough to drink!) so we wanted their reward to be something useful and exciting to them. Had we defaulted to just wine or just chocolates, it may have left our people still feeling unappreciated as we didn't take their personal preference into consideration! Bottom line, know your people, know what will make them feel appreciated, and what won't.

Rule 2 – Make appreciation unified

The next golden rule, the letter "U," focuses on **appreciating your people in a unified and inclusive manner**. Appreciation does not – and should not – create a divide or wedge between your people, with the "haves" and "have nots." Instead, appreciation needs to be universal so everyone can receive it. I say this because too often we focus our appreciation on certain people or groups, or put limits on who can be recognized. And when this happens, you risk your people feeling excluded, feeling resentful, and ultimately missing out on all of the superpowers of appreciation. Here are three things to do to help you show appreciation in a unified and inclusive way:

1. **Put on your appreciation "glasses"** – The starting point is to look for opportunities to show appreciation everywhere and anywhere. In training classes I often say that we all need to put our appreciation "glasses" on, thus looking for and seeking out opportunities to appreciate our people. This is absolutely critical, for if you don't first see the moments, then they will be missed, and the appreciation will never happen.

   Consider times when your people have done quality work, have suggested new ideas, have learned a new skill, have hit a milestone or achieved an objective, have supported a colleague or customer, or have shown teamwork or cooperation. The list is endless once you put on your appreciation glasses!

Catch me if you can

When we were going through the adoption process, we had to go through a series of classes. At one they told us something that has stuck with me when it comes to our children, but also when it comes to appreciation. They said that it is important to "catch your children being good, don't anxiously wait for them to be bad." Be on the lookout to catch your people doing something good and great, and then appreciate it!

---

2. **Remember your "glue people"** – Every organization has what Eric Hutcherson, Chief People & Inclusion Officer at Universal Group, calls his "glue people." He explained that when he was at the National Basketball Association they had their stars and their glue people, those that held the team

together. He went on to say that if they only recognized their stars, or in basketball terms, their scorers, they were completely ignoring those that make the assists or grab the rebounds or play great defense. These people, your glue people, are the ones that day after day show up and contribute to the success of your company, and deserve appreciation just as much as the star players.

3. **Adopt a "crowdsourcing" approach** – And finally, if you want to show appreciation in a unified and inclusive way, you can't do it alone – after all, you can't be everywhere at once! You can adopt a "crowdsourcing" approach to appreciation and enlist the help of your people to help capture all of the appreciation moments, while encouraging your people to work together and form a collective responsibility for it.

Rule 3 – Shine a spotlight on appreciation

Let's next move on to the letter "S," which stands for **shining a spotlight on appreciation**. In the past, it was done in a very private way, between the sender and the receiver, but over the years we've come to see the importance of changing this to put it under the spotlight and watch the magic happen. The benefits are that it showcases what good and great look like to your people and what will lead to being recognized, it multiplies the impact as others see and get involved with the appreciation, and it connects your people in a positive, meaningful, and uplifting way. It's like having cheerleaders to celebrate and release more of those appreciation happiness chemicals!

An example from Ken is when he used crowdsourcing to improve appreciation at his previous company:

First, I set up a channel in our company's social media platform solely devoted to appreciation, calling it "Kudos." Here anyone and everyone could send appreciation messages to one another, and because it was a social platform, people could get involved by commenting and using emojis to further show appreciation to colleagues. And since doing this was far from natural for my engineers, during weekly 1:1 meetings with my people I would end by asking if anyone had done something worth appreciating, and then encouraging them to post it in the Kudos channel. This helped my people understand why, when, and how to show appreciation, and also gave me greater visibility of what my people were doing so that I in turn could show them appreciation.

Rule 4 – Make appreciation timely

The last letter of the acronym is "T," which stands for **making appreciation timely,** and focuses on the "when" of showing appreciation. This can confuse people, as what is an "appropriate time frame," really? Does it mean giving appreciation once a week, once a month? I propose that instead, we focus the definition and our efforts on the gap, the time frame between the moment the behavior or action happens and the moment the appreciation occurs.

Why wait until a certain day of the week or month to show appreciation, why not give it now before you forget AND the impact of the recognition wears off?

I describe timely appreciation as "putting the foot on the accelerator." To explain this, let me ask you a question – if you were on a highway and the speed limit was 70 miles per hour, would you go this speed? The obvious answer is yes, as long as it's safe to do so. What does this have to do with appreciation? Well, if showing appreciation creates these superpowers we mentioned earlier, making them more motivated, productive, etc., would you want to wait on these powers? Of course you wouldn't, which means that by giving timely appreciation to your people they can put their foot on the accelerator. And, more importantly, keep their "car" – your company – driving forward.

Here are two things you can do to make your appreciation more timely:

1. **Aim for "in the moment" appreciation** – You can be more deliberate about giving "in the moment" appreciation," which is when there is little to no gap between the contribution and when you show appreciation. If you can't give the appreciation that very moment, consider practicing "in the moment" note taking, jotting down the contributions so that you don't forget these meaningful moments.

2. **Appreciate small wins** – A key element of "in the moment" appreciation is recognizing the small wins, not just the big, end results. Here's a lovely story from the book *Leading with Gratitude* that illustrates this concept:

   "Former Ford chief Alan Mulally explained to us that rewarding small wins shows that a leader knows what's going on. In his weekly business plan review, each member of his leadership team was expected to present a color-coded update of his or her progress toward meeting key company goals. When someone shows a red, we say, 'Thank you for that visibility.' When we work a red to a yellow, we thank everybody. Celebrations for each step show the team that it's expected behavior to make progress. People are feeling 'Wow. I'm needed. I'm supported.'"

NEXT STEPS

☐ Talk to your people about their appreciation preferences, e.g. how do they like to be shown appreciation? What's important to them? Take notes so you can use these findings when you give them appreciation next!

☐ Make appreciation a habit with deliberate actions. This could be setting up a file to jot down times when you spot someone doing something worthy of appreciation, and then sitting down once a week to send out appreciation. Or, you can be more deliberate about your "in the moment" appreciation. Try out a few ways, talk to others to see how they do it, and come up with an approach that will work for you.

☐ Think of how you'll track your appreciation, keeping an eye on who, when, and what you are appreciating. This will help you share and celebrate these moments with your people, but also help ensure your appreciation is inclusive to capture everyone's contributions, especially "glue people."

DEVELOPMENT

Key Building Block for the Avoider, the Hoarder, the Blocker, and the Micromanager

The next two building blocks, Development and Coaching, are sometimes used interchangeably. However, although they are related, working towards similar goals, they are different in how they get there. One way to think of it is that with development you **give your people a map** that sets out where they need to go, whereas with coaching you **help your people draw their own map**.

That being said, there's often blurred lines and overlap between them, which can cause some debate. Personally, I don't care what you call it as long as at its core you focus on the goal – which is helping your people be and do their best work by learning, developing, growing, and becoming more confident. They're part of a paint palette, and ready for you to blend them together over and over again to help create your masterpiece, your people!

> "We're not here to mark your paper, we're here to help you get an A, because life's not about some normal distribution curve. It's about helping people get A's." — *Garry Ridge, author, Chairman Emeritus WD-40 Company*

WHY IT MATTERS

Over the years, more emphasis and focus has been put on the development of our people as we've come under the pressure to upskill and reskill them to meet the changing needs of the workplace and our businesses. But it's also become more critical to our people, with one survey[60] finding that development moved from the ninth most important driver of a great work culture to **the top driver of culture** in just two years.

Another study[61] shows how development influences both attraction and retention:

- **Higher employee attraction** – Almost all (92%) of job candidates consider learning and development opportunities as a deciding factor when considering job offers from two employers.

- **Higher employee retention** – 86% of respondents expressed a willingness to stay longer with their company if they offered more learning and development opportunities.

> **"Train people well so they can leave. Treat them well enough so they don't want to."** — *Sir Richard Branson, Founder of Virgin Group*

ACTIONS TO TAKE

One survey[62] found that almost all employees (91%) believe that it's important for their boss to inspire their learning and experimentation. So it's obvious that this needs to be a big building block to work on for your people, but how do you get it right? Let's get into a little more detail to get you on your way.

---

60   Glint, Well-Being report, 2021.

61   IMC report, 2023.

62   LinkedIn, Skills Advantage report, 2022.

Put in the work

The first thing to say is that there is not just one way to develop your people. You can't send all of them on one magic training course, and bang, they're "finished"! And that's because development is not one-dimensional, there are many factors that impact how you develop your people. It depends on the person, how they like to learn, where they want to go, etc. That's why you need to put in the work to make it work.

Here are four questions that I ask my people when working with them on their development plan, which helps us formulate their developmental goals and "give them the map" to help them achieve them.

1. **Where are you now?** – What are my strong skills? Go on, celebrate these!

2. **Where do I need to be in the short term?** – What skills and experience do I need so I can do my current job better?

3. **Where do I need to be in the long term?** – What skills and experience do I need to achieve my future career aspirations?

4. **How do I like to learn and develop?** – What are my preferred ways to develop, e.g. take classes, attend conferences, read books, listen to videos, shadow someone, be mentored?

In respect to the fourth question, although every person is different, there is an interesting model that comes from research done by McCall, Lombardo, and Eichinger that talks about how people often learn and develop. It's called the 70-20-10 model, and it says that:

- 70% of learning happens through on-the-job experience

- 20% of learning happens socially through colleagues and friends

- 10% of learning happens via formal training experiences

And while I'm not saying that you should strictly use these percentages, I do believe that they act as helpful guidelines. They also remind you that a mix of learning tools and approaches is best for building a balanced and effective plan for individuals. Personalize it based on how your people answer the questions, creating what is right for them.

Pat explained to their boss that they were "hungry for progression and promotion." Together they worked out how Pat could achieve these goals, working their way up the agreed career path. When Pat would reach one peak, their boss would offer another opportunity to learn and grow, from going back to school to gain a degree to being sent to relocate to another division. As Pat explained, "This was a huge achievement for me, and I was very grateful for the support my boss gave me, giving me the support and flexibility to reach my goals."

Shift the power

One of the main reasons the Development building block can crumble is when you push, force, or threaten your people to learn, where learning is something you do "to" your people. "You must attend this class, you must take this workshop," the list goes on and on. Trust me, this doesn't work, because at the end of the day, only your people can decide if they're going to "show up" for learning. You can't force them to do this!

At a previous company we learned this particular lesson when we re-launched our in-house Training Academy. We came up with a traditional matrix of courses that were mandatory, and it just didn't work. We were spending tons of time trying to get people to take these classes, but in the end, we nixed the idea. We made a few courses mandatory, such as those relating to security, but besides this, we let employees decide which ones were useful to them depending on what they needed, what challenges they were facing, and the ambitions or interests they had for themselves.

You need to shift the power and let your people own their development. After all, they're the one that will care the most! So although you can help them by making tools and resources available, and being there for them along the way, ultimately your people must own their learning journey.

Treat it like a journey

And speaking of a journey, that is what their "development map," or plan, really is, with many things that need to be done along the way if you want your people to reach their "destination." Think of yourself acting like a GPS that's constantly looking for better routes to go as things change. How can you help your people constantly reassess how they're doing, and then calibrate and adjust the plan accordingly? Do this on a regular basis by integrating it into your regular conversations and making it a normal and ongoing dialogue. This not only ensures that your people stay on track and achieve their goals, but it helps you be a better boss in supporting their development.

Another part of the journey involves "losing the swim lanes." What I mean by this is that in the past, jobs were designed in swim lanes – nice and neat; you do your job and I do mine. But based on changes in how we do business and how we do our jobs, the lane separators have been widened or removed, with our workforce and their jobs swimming in a more integrated way. Take notice of how your people move between lanes, and how this ultimately impacts their development plan.

Encourage stepping out of comfort zones

We're all human, which means that sometimes we want to take the easy route and stick to things that we're good at. But when it comes to development, you must be willing to take that step out of your comfort zone, confronting things that may be scary and uncomfortable.

As a boss, this is something you need to do to help your people, giving them a nudge to try their hand at a new task or learn something new. These little nudges can show them the benefits of learning new things, how they'll grow and reach new goals, but also build their self-confidence. Think about how this can show them that they are brave and capable, facing and overcoming their fears.

That being said, as I'm sure you've found yourself, sometimes trying something new involves failure, or as we called them earlier in the book, "learning moments." When you encourage people to step out of their comfort zone, mention these learning moments, so they know that you'll support them if and when this happens to them. Remember the "Yeah we failed" Slack channel? Own your learning moments!

Supersize It

In Liz Wiseman's book titled *Multipliers*, she shares an exercise called "Supersize It." You begin by thinking about how you'd buy shoes for a young child, buying that one size too big so that they can grow into it. And if/when they complain, you say to them, "Don't worry, you'll grow into them."

Wiseman says, "Try supersizing someone's job. Assess their current capabilities and then give them a challenge that is a size too big. Give an individual contributor a leadership role; give a first-line manager more decision-making power. If they seem startled, acknowledge that the role or responsibility might feel awkward at first. Then step back and watch them grow into it."

NEXT STEPS

☐ Talk to your people about their development preferences, such as how they learn best or what they want to learn, so that you can create the best approach and plan for them.

☐ Map out a development plan with each of your people, including where they want to be in the short and long term. Make sure to include some kind of supersize or stretch goal, something to move them out of their comfort zone to learn in different ways.

☐ Build development conversations into your regular meetings with your people, so that you both can own and drive it.

COACHING

Key Building Block for the Unappreciater, the Pretender, the Blocker, and the Micromanager

I've been lucky enough to have some great coaches over the years, both in the workplace and as a competitive gymnast. And although they coached me in different ways and for different reasons, they all had profound and lasting impacts on me professionally and personally. The common theme was that they supported and drove me to wonderful places that were sometimes completely outside of my comfort zone or beyond my wildest imagination (e.g. a double backflip for the first time or presenting in front of a Board of Directors).

The magic is how they did it, rather, how they got *me* to do it. They weren't the one flying through the air doing the double backflip or standing in front of the Board of Directors, I was. But as my coach, they were the ones who helped me find the answers, unlocking my potential and supporting me in getting there.

> **"Coaching is an on-call business. It's a dialogue-based relationship, you need to know where your people are in real-time."** — *Coach Dana Cavalea, leadership coach, author and former New York Yankees Performance Coach*

The focus on coaching has increased over the years as we learn the difference it can make to our people. This is actually the main reason we decided to give it its own building block, separating it from Development. Here's an excerpt from an article[63] by Herminia

---

63   Herminia Ibarra and Anne Scoular, Harvard Business Review, *The Leader as Coach*, 2019.

Ibarra and Anne Scoular appearing in the Harvard Business Review that explains this, "Twenty-first-century managers simply don't (and can't!) have all the right answers. To cope with this new reality, companies are moving away from traditional command-and-control practices and toward something very different: a model in which managers give support and guidance rather than instructions, and employees learn how to adapt to constantly changing environments in ways that unleash fresh energy, innovation, and commitment. The role of the manager, in short, is becoming that of a coach."

What's in a name?

At WD-40 they made the decision to change the title for their managers to that of coach. Here's what Garry Ridge, former CEO at WD-40 said about this:

"I looked at the indigenous Australians and the Fiji and Islanders. One of the things that came out really strong was that the number one responsibility of a tribal leader is to be a learner and a teacher. That's what I think the number one responsibility of a leader is, is to be a learner and a teacher, to help his people or her people step into the best version of their personal self.

That's why we call our managers here coaches, not managers, because a coach's job is not to run on the field and play on the team on the game, it's to stand in the locker room and on the sidelines and to be observing the game, looking for plays, and coaching them into their best plays."

WHY IT MATTERS

To stay ahead of their competition, companies are constantly looking for ways to enhance employee performance, foster growth, and achieve better business results. Coaching has been proven to support all of these and more, going beyond traditional development practices to help their people (and business) reach their full potential.

According to one study,[64] companies with strong coaching cultures report higher employee engagement and performance. Specifically, they found that 60% of companies with strong coaching cultures reported above-average employee engagement, while only 36% of companies without coaching cultures reported the same. They also found that organizations with strong coaching cultures had 47% higher revenue per employee than those without.

Here's a bit more about the positive impacts of coaching:

- **Increased self-confidence** – According to one survey,[65] 80% of people who receive coaching report increased self-confidence.

- **Higher employee retention** – According to this same survey, organizations with a strong coaching culture have a 40% higher employee retention rate.

- **Higher performance** – In another study,[66] companies with high-quality coaching programs reported an increase in productivity, as reported by 80% of survey respondents.

- **Improved wellbeing** – The results of another study[67] suggest that the application of coaching in the workplace improves employee wellbeing and performance.

- **Higher employee engagement** – According to a Gallup study,[68] organizations with a strong coaching culture have 60% higher employee engagement compared to those without it.

---

64   HCI and ICF study, *Building Strong Coaching Cultures for the Future*, 2019.
65   ICF study, 2009.
66   CIPD, Good Work Index, 2022.
67   Joanna Jarosz, *The impact of coaching on well-being and performance of managers and their teams during pandemic*, 2021.
68   Aldona Oleńkiewicz, *Why It's Worth Installing a Coaching Culture in Your Organization?*, 2023.

ACTIONS TO TAKE

As we've just shown, coaching can have many positive effects for your people and your business. However, coaching is often misunderstood and used incorrectly. Next, we'll explore some actions to help you get it right, acting as a coach in ways that will truly get the best out of your people.

Coaching is a process

Unfortunately, as nice as it would be, coaching is not one simple step or action, but rather it is a process to equip your people with the knowledge, tools, and opportunities they need to succeed and give them control over their development. A process that is widely used is the GROW model, developed by Sir John Whitmore, and described in his book, *Coaching for Performance*. The acronym **GROW** stands for **G**oal, **R**eality, **O**ptions, and **W**ill. It's a simple and structured process that you can use for a variety of different types of coaching scenarios, e.g. career development, performance improvement, personal growth, etc.

The key to this model, as with coaching in general, is to ask open-ended questions that help your coachee *explore options, generate ideas*, and *commit to actions* to help them achieve their goals. Here's a high-level summary of each of the four steps:

1. **Goal** – The step is all about goal setting, determining the outcome of the coaching sessions. This is where you ask questions to help your coachee begin with the end in mind. When doing this, I often ask my people to picture our last session together, asking them what we'll be celebrating, what have they achieved? By doing this it provides focus, identifying what they want to achieve, and putting them on the path to accomplishing it by focusing on the solution rather than the problem.

2. **Reality –** The step involves exploring your coachee's reality, what is their world like at the moment? Use this step to ask questions about their current situation, and to identify any challenges, obstacles, issues, or gaps that exist that may get in the way of reaching their goals. This step is part of what differentiates coaching from normal development conversation, where we tend to go straight from the past to the future.

3. **Options –** Next, it's time to explore what your coachee can do to move forward to achieve their goals. This involves helping them to think broadly and deeply to explore all options, ones they've considered and possibly never considered as you help them push past and through some of their reservations and doubts. In one article[69], they suggested asking the question, "If you had a magic wand, what would you do?" I love this because it does open the door and their mind to all possibilities.

4. **Will –** The last step is where you help your coachee wrap things up, helping them determine what actions they need to take to move forward and achieve their goals. Over the years, some have changed this last step, but Whitmore was unequivocal in his explanation that W stood for "will" in the sense of having the will to commit. Whatever you decide to name it, the key here is deciding and setting out a plan of which options and actions are to be taken forward. It's also important that you help them choose options that are actionable, e.g. will work for them. For example, if a person commits to joining a gym because they want to lose weight, but hate going to gym, it would be more beneficial for them to commit to doing something they enjoy, like walking their dog.

---

69   Herminia Ibarra and Anne Scoular, Harvard Business Review, *The Leader as Coach*, 2019.

Be silent and patient

I love coaching people, but I have to be honest and say that it didn't come naturally for me. And that's because my natural style and approach is to present ideas, give people guidance and, yes, tell people what to do. I did this because I believed they wanted and needed this (sound familiar to some of the Micromanager traits?). But with coaching, this is exactly what you don't want to do, instead silently and patiently letting the learner arrive with their own answers.

When I was in high school, I helped out at the gym where I trained to coach the little ones. I would show them how to do a skill, let's say a somersault on the balance beam, and then ask them to do the skill themselves. And do you know what? One by one they got it wrong! I was befuddled, "Why couldn't they just do what I had demonstrated to them?" The reality, as my boss explained, was that they would only learn if they tried it themselves to understand how they needed to do it differently, rather than just watching how I did it.

Coaching is all about drawing wisdom, insights, and creativity out of your people, letting them discover solutions on their own. Going back to my gymnastics example, it's about letting your people learn how to somersault on their own. Remember to:

- **Ask questions** – Hold back from providing and presenting answers, instead ask questions to guide them to come up with their own answers, not yours.

- **Be patient** – The trick to coaching is to be patient, letting the conversation go where it goes. Remind yourself that sometimes you need to go in a different direction to get to the end, which is perfectly okay.

- **Relinquish control** – It's equally important to relinquish control to your people, empowering them and giving them ownership. By doing this, they own the action plan and feel more committed to it.

"Coaching is being able to facilitate the moments of insight in a person. Hold the silence to give them the time to answer or figure it out and ask yourself – how can I turn something into a question rather than give them a solution?" — *Clare Edwards, BrainSmart People Development*

You don't need to know everything

Another lesson I've learned about coaching is that you don't have to have all the answers, and you don't have to have done it yourself. To illustrate this, let me tell you about two of my favorite coaches, one real and one fictional.

The real one is Valorie Kondos Field or "Miss Val," who although retired, is still regarded as one of the most accomplished U.S. collegiate gymnastics coaches of all time. During her 28 years as head coach of the UCLA women's gymnastics team, she brought home an amazing seven national and 18 PAC-12 championships. And here's the kicker: She never did gymnastics herself, she was actually a dancer!

The fictional coach is Ted Lasso, star of the television show of the same name. He was an American who had coached American football, and moved to the U.K. to coach British football ("soccer" as they call it in the U.S.). And although Lasso didn't have the success that Field did, his successes in the locker room and as a role model to his players and other coaches were unprecedented. And yet, he never played the game himself. In fact, throughout the show, there are amusing scenes of when he didn't understand the sport.

What they both lacked in knowledge of the sports they made up for in their amazing skills as coaches. **Coaching isn't about "playing an instrument," it's about being a great conductor, helping your people play and perform the most beautiful music.**

This happened to both of us, when I took on responsibility for Payroll having no prior experience managing this important function, and likewise, Ken took on responsibility for an Android mobile app team. At first it felt overwhelming, having a bit of "imposter syndrome," but soon we realized that as a coach we could help our people learn and grow in meaningful and lasting ways. And as an extra bonus, we both learned some new skills ourselves!

NEXT STEPS

☐ Talk to your people to find out what kind of coaching they need, and what approach works best for them.

☐ What can you do to develop your coaching skills, taking on board the tips and actions shared in this section?

☐ Think back to a time when you had someone coach you, either in work or in your personal life. What made this approach to development work well? How can you incorporate these lessons into how you coach your people?

EMPOWERMENT

Key Building Block for the Pretender, the Firefighter, and the Micromanager

Our world is constantly evolving, with rapid changes in technology and the need to support increasingly global markets, while outrunning our competition as best we can. As bosses, we have no choice but to adapt how we lead our people so that we can deal with our environment, team, and challenges in a more agile, adaptable, and resilient way.

Key to this is the concept of Empowerment, one of our last building blocks, which is about giving your people the freedom, power, control, and space to take ownership of their work. Bosses who empower their people **focus on support instead of micromanaging**, giving their people autonomy to make in-the-moment and on-the-ground decisions. This not only helps you move quicker but helps your people grow their skills and confidence to reach their full potential. And with more companies adopting flexible work arrangements and patterns, and a lack of "eyes" on your people, the need has never been greater.

Empowerment is about letting your people stand in their own "space" and not crowding them with your presence.

This concept is brought to life in General Stanley McChrystal's book *Team of Teams*, where he chronicles his efforts as Commander of the U.S. Joint Special Operations Task Force in Iraq. He talks about an initiative he called the "empowered execution," and the tremendous success it had when they flipped the switch from micromanaging to empowerment:

"I began to reconsider the nature of my role as a leader. The wait for my approval was not resulting in any better decisions, and our priority should be reaching the best possible decision that could be made in a time frame that allowed it to be relevant. I came to realize that, in normal cases, I did not add tremendous value, so I changed the process. The risks of acting too slowly were higher than the risks of letting competent people make judgment calls. Our teams were crafted to be chess pieces with well-honed, predictable capabilities. Our leaders, including me, had been trained as chess masters, and we hoped to display the talent and skill of masters. We felt responsible, and harbored a corresponding need to be in control, but as we were learning, we actually needed to let go."

Empowerment versus autonomy

These words are often used in the same sentence, which can be confusing when determining their separate meanings. Our thoughts are that **empowerment is the process**, and **autonomy is the destination**. Empowerment is what you as a boss give, and autonomy is what your person receives in return.

WHY IT MATTERS

Employees who are empowered have been proven to have stronger job performance, higher trust, higher job satisfaction, and greater commitment to their company. In fact, according to one study,[70] nearly half of respondents said they'd give up a 20% raise for greater control over how they work, proving the importance of autonomy.

Empowered employees are also more likely to be engaged at work. One study[71] found that empowered employees rank in the 79th percentile of employee engagement, while disempowered employees rank in the 24th percentile.

---

70   PwC, *Secure your future people experience*, 2019.
71   Joseph Folkman, 2019.

A lot of this has to do with the impact empowerment and autonomy has on motivation. According to the self-determination theory (SDT), which was developed by two American psychologists, Richard Ryan and Edward Deci, intrinsic motivation is the "foundational catalyst of human success and fulfillment." Their theory challenged the prevailing belief that reward is the main driver of motivation in humans, saying that instead self-determination, which is made up of three components: autonomy, competence, and relatedness, actually drives motivation.

I've seen this theory in practice time and time again, with my people being more motivated when I empower them and give them more autonomy. That's because they feel more confident, knowing that I've entrusted them to grab the reins, which leads to them having a greater sense of pride, satisfaction, and ownership with their work and the company. Empowering your people can greatly benefit your company, leading to better results and success.

ACTIONS TO TAKE

How hard can empowerment be? All you're doing is passing the baton to your people, giving them more power and control, right?! Yes, but it's far from a simple act, which is why in our survey eight out of 10 participants said that they've had a boss who was a Micromanager, someone who doesn't empower their people. But, as with our other building blocks, you can get better at Empowerment with a little guidance. Let's get started.

Begin with shared consciousness

The absolute starting point, and the foundation for empowerment is something called "shared consciousness," which can be defined as common ideas, attitudes, and beliefs. In the corporate world, these are your company's mission, purpose, and values, and they are your shared consciousness as they work together to explain to your people **where your business is going**, and the **actions and behaviors that will help you get there**.

Think of your mission and purpose as your north star, clearly showing you and your people where you're trying to get to, and your values as your map, helping you get there. In the absence of a boss (you), you want to make sure your people understand your company's north star and map so they don't aimlessly make decisions or take actions that don't fulfill your company's mission and purpose.

This means that your people must be absolutely clear on what your mission, purpose, and values are, and also what they are not. Embed your company values into everything that you as a boss does, and encourage your people to do the same, particularly when it comes to making decisions. Set your people up for success by showing them how to put values at the core of every business action to drive forward the company's mission and purpose.

An example of this is U.S. online retailer Zappos's approach to empowerment, using their mission and values as a guide. Their mission is a simple one, to "provide the best customer service possible," but they deliver on this by encouraging employees to take ownership of customer interactions and to make decisions that lead to the best outcomes for them, to achieve their mission.

I heard this firsthand when I had the opportunity to visit Zappos's head office for research on a previous book, and I spoke to a member of their help desk team. They told me of how they owned a customer situation, delivering on the mission and living their company value of "Deliver WOW Through Service."

The situation was a customer calling to return her bridesmaid dresses because her fiance had canceled the wedding a week before the big day. Instead of just telling the customer the process to follow, she recognized the needs of the customer and did something about it by helping her return the dresses and then sending her a spa voucher with a handwritten note saying "I know you're going through a hard time, so do something special for yourself." By truly owning the situation and thinking about how to deliver on Zappos's values, you can be sure that she made the company mission shine and felt a sense of empowerment!

Empowerment stems from trust

Another foundation of Empowerment is Trust, one of the other building blocks. If you think back to some of the bad bosses where empowerment is not happening, e.g. Micromanager, Hoarder, Coercer, a great deal of this has to do with a lack of trust in their people and thus closely controlling why, when, and how they do their jobs.

When thinking about trust in respect to empowerment, I like to describe it in two ways. The first has to do with trusting your people in *what they do*, e.g. how they get their work done. The second involves trusting your people to *come to you* if and when they need your support. They are equally important and need to be described and discussed upfront when you empower your people.

I had empowered one of my people to prepare and present a proposal for a new program to our Board of Directors. I supported her as she prepared for it, and as we went into the board room I told her that I trusted her completely in doing a fantastic job, but that if at any time she felt she needed me to jump in to just let me know. This conversation showed that I trusted her, but I also had her back. I'm pleased (and proud) to say that she did a brilliant job, with me quietly sitting in the background.

If your Empowerment building block is ever going to work, the bottom line is that you have to trust your people. And if you don't trust them, it's time to take a step back and ask yourself why this is the case. You may want to go back and read the Trust building block for more tips on this.

"Leadership is about empowering other people as a result of your presence and making sure that impact continues into your absence." — *Frances Frei, author of Unleashed*

Empower outcomes, not activities

Besides trust, another problem I see time and time again when it comes to empowerment has to do with the "what." Too often bosses think that to tick the empowerment box, they merely carve out a few individual tasks or activities, and presto, their people will feel like they have autonomy. Well, sorry to burst their bubble, but this isn't how it works. It can feel belittling and potentially even piss your people off!

Instead, empower your people to act against the outcome (your goal) in three ways. First, bring them in at the start to *determine the outcome*, e.g. what are we trying to achieve, what does success look like? Next, have them *identify the activities* that will get them to the outcome. And finally, have them take ownership in *achieving the activities*. This can feel daunting as it can be hard to lose control, see people do things differently than you, and even make mistakes. But remind yourself of the benefits of empowerment and that mistakes, learning moments, will only help your people grow and develop. By empowering outcomes instead of activities you help your people understand and discover new ways of achieving goals that they may not have had access to before, helping them in the short and long term.

Tend your garden

It's important to note that your empowerment should not lead to neglect. What I mean by this is that you don't just empower your people and then, like the Avoider boss, disappear, leaving them alone to "get on with things." As I did with my direct report, as a boss, you need to have your people's backs, especially as they take on new responsibilities and are tasked with achieving new outcomes.

In McChrystal's book *Team of Teams*, he uses a garden analogy to explain this. And since we love analogies, let me share this with you: "Gardeners plant and harvest, but more than anything, they tend. Plants are watered, beds are fertilized, and weeds are removed. They understand that by doing this, their plants and crops grow stronger." The same is true when empowering your people, you need to "tend them," giving them the water, nutrients, and support they need over and over again, especially when you're empowering them.

Here are a few things to keep in mind as you tend your garden:

- **Provide tools and resources –** Going back to the Zappos example where employees were given autonomy to handle situations with customers, the only reason it worked is because they were given tools and resources they needed to make informed decisions. This is critical to do, to set your people up with what they need to achieve their agreed outcomes.

- **Give feedback –** Equally important is to give your people continuous feedback, helping them understand what's working and opportunities for improvement throughout the process. In a story shared with you earlier, my boss empowered me to do a six-month project and then gave me no feedback, leading to me feeling like I failed, and the project incomplete. Sure, they empowered me, but then I was left on my own.

- **Be present –** In the military they use the term "battlefield circulation," which is when you go out and visit your locations and units. This concept of being present, whether it's literally or figuratively, is pivotal when it comes to empowerment. Your people need to know that even though they have autonomy for their work, you're there for them and present to help them deal with any problems or issues they may face, stepping in to help remove roadblocks and any other obstacles in their way.

- **Don't send them out injured** – This next concept is something I discussed with Coach Dana Cavalea, former coach of the New York Yankees. He explained that if a player is injured, you don't send them out to play a game, you give them time to recover. Likewise, you need to understand if your people are "injured," or unprepared, for the task at hand. If they need more preparation, such as being upskilled or extra coaching, don't put them in the "game" until they're ready!

- **Don't be afraid to pull the emergency brake** – And finally, if things get bad and you're seeing problems occur, don't be afraid to "pull the emergency brake" and jump in. This concept came about when I was teaching my daughter to drive a car, giving her autonomy as she was in the driver's seat. At one point in time, we were almost ready to crash into the back of another car and as much as I wanted her to own the situation, I had to pull the emergency brake to save us and the other driver. Of course, this should be a last resort, but it can be necessary.

Align with what your people need

As we've mentioned numerous times throughout the book, every person is different, having different needs and preferred ways of doing their work, and working with you. This impacts how you empower your people, as different people need or prefer different things. In one article,[72] they call this the "rhythm of involvement," saying that it varies "depending on whether employees need intensive *guidance* in the short term or intermittent *path clearing* over a prolonged period."

---

72   Colin M. Fisher, Teresa M. Amabile, and Julianna Pillemer, Harvard Business Review, *How to Help (Without Micromanaging)*, 2021.

I've seen this with my people, with some wanting what I'd call high-touch empowerment, checking in with me and requiring my guidance quite often, and others preferring low touch, only coming to me if/when they need me, and others having a mix of both. As a boss, it's your job to discuss and agree on these definitions and ways of working together upfront, and doing so continually as work and circumstances change. Getting this right can be the difference between giving the gift of autonomy, and being seen as a micromanager … you choose which you'd prefer!

Sometimes empowerment is standing in the back

When I interviewed Andrew Follows, Managing Director at Aquilae, he shared with me a lovely story that talks about the power of empowerment, and what we can learn by moving from the front to the back.

When I was 19 years old, during my vacation from university in the U.K., I took a job with an organization that organized English language safaris for French children aged around 10 to 14. We spent the mornings in the classrooms teaching the children English, and in the afternoons we took them out on excursions. One of these excursions involved walks through the local countryside, which was lovely until we had to cross a busy highway. I'd make sure I reached it first, and then I'd turn into a mother hen with all my chicks trying to get them safely across the four-lane highway. They would continue talking with each other, generally messing about, and entrust to me the whole operation of getting them safely to the other side.

On one occasion something else must have taken my attention, and as the group came to the road I found myself right at the back. When they reached the road without me up front, the kids stopped walking, stopped talking, started looking both ways very intentionally, and focused on getting themselves and each other safely across it. From then on, I always made a point of hanging back and letting the group in my care take responsibility for getting themselves across the road. And, I'm proud to say I didn't lose a single child on that road, and I was invited back to facilitate the program the following year.

NEXT STEPS

☐ Remind yourself that you hired your people because of the skills and talents that they brought to you and the company. How can you leverage these to give them more ownership and empowerment? How can you ensure you're focusing on the outcome and not the activities?

☐ Talk to your people to find out what empowerment means to them. How much or how little guidance do they prefer, and does this change based on the work and responsibilities?

☐ Think back to a time when you used your authority to get things done. What impact did this have on your people and the end results? What lessons can you learn from this to show less authority and more empowerment going forward?

INSPIRATION

Key Building Block for the Unappreciater, the Blocker and the Firefighter

The final building block is Inspiration. It's a great one to end on as it's so positive and uplifting, and because of the impact it can have on other building blocks, enabling and supporting them (e.g. inspired people can be more open to Feedback, Communication, Appreciation, etc.).

Inspiration is the invisible fuel that motivates and powers your people. It's the catalyst that transforms mundane tasks into meaningful endeavors, elevating the collective spirit and driving everyone toward a common goal. When a team is inspired, the atmosphere is electric – ideas flow freely, collaboration is effortless, and challenges are met with enthusiasm rather than dread. It can be that magic ingredient that can propel a project from mediocrity to excellence, and it's often the distinguishing factor between teams and companies that merely function and those that truly thrive and succeed.

However, the pursuit of inspiration is not without its complexities. For one thing, you cannot force people to be inspired, they need to be receptive and open-minded to it. Next, just like Respect or Trust, it can disappear in a moment, so there's a need to continually nurture this block with your people. And finally, if done wrong it can inadvertently lead to burnout or neglect of your people's needs as you're focusing more on the end game than them.

> **"The most important thing is to try and inspire people so that they can be great in whatever they want to do."** — *Kobe Bryant, former American basketball player*

WHY IT MATTERS

Having an inspired workforce is absolutely critical to your business for a variety of reasons. First, it can lead to higher levels of engagement and performance as your people are more likely to be emotionally invested in their work and the success of the company. Next, it can be a driving force behind innovation and unlocking creativity, as inspired people are more likely to think outside the box and challenge the status quo. This kind of thinking can lead to truly groundbreaking ideas and solutions that can set your company apart from your competitors. And finally, inspiration can foster a positive work environment as inspired teams are generally happier, more motivated, cohesive, and collaborative. Add this all together, and your people have higher job satisfaction, while your business will have lower turnover and be more successful.

"Inspiration awakens us to new possibilities by allowing us to transcend our ordinary experiences and limitations. Inspiration propels a person from apathy to possibility, and transforms the way we perceive our own capabilities." — *Scott Barry Kaufman*

To add to this, research[73] done by psychologists Todd M. Thrash and Andrew J. Elliot found that inspired people were more open to new experiences, reported more absorption in their tasks, and had a stronger drive to master their work. Plus, inspired people were more intrinsically motivated and less extrinsically motivated, which impacts work performance.

---

73   Scott Barry Kaufman, Scientific American, *From Evaluation to Inspiration*, 2014.

ACTIONS TO TAKE

When people think of an inspirational leader they often think of that charismatic and energetic person who stands on stage, moving and motivating the audience. And while in the moment they may be inspirational, true inspiration is a more long-term goal and requirement of a great boss. If you can inspire your people, then they'll be with you for the long haul. Here are a few ideas on how you can shape your own inspiration.

Be purpose-driven

Inspiration begins with intent, having something for you and your people to believe in and work towards, a common purpose. Earlier in the book we described this as your "north star," shining brightly to motivate and guide your people through the fast-paced, complex, and ever-changing "sky," the world we work in. Defining your north star helps drive your people not just for the short-term, but in the long-term, giving them the energy and focus to safely and effectively get where they (and you) need to go.

One of my favorite stories to bring this concept to life is from the book *Will it Make the Boat Go Faster* by Harriet Beveridge and Ben Hunt-Davis. In it, they tell the story of how the British Olympic rowing team in 2000 had used one single question, "Will it make the boat go faster?" as their purpose to help them win an Olympic gold medal. They were inspired and driven by an uncompromising focus on this question, making it a non-negotiable in every decision they made, from how a training session should be run, to what they should eat, to how much sleep they should get. Over a two-year period, this method improved the team's performance, gave them a competitive advantage, and ultimately helped them achieve their mission.

What I love about this story is that the British team were the underdogs (who doesn't love an underdog, right?). If you listen to the commentator you'll hear that up until the very end of the race he expected them to crash and burn, and to lose the lead they'd maintained throughout the race. But inspired by their uncompromising focus on their mission and purpose of winning gold through their commitment to their one question, they surprised the world and won.

In practice, being purpose-driven is being clear on what your purpose is, and what it does and doesn't mean. You need to believe in it enough that you become uncompromising in living and driving it through your decisions, actions and behaviors. And, lastly, you need to continually reinforce it through your other building blocks.

Be clear on expectations

Purpose alone is not enough to inspire your people. Think of the rowing team, who were training for two years to get to the Olympics. Although driven by their purpose, they needed shorter-term goals and objectives or they never would have made it to (or won) the race.

The same is true with your people. If you want them to be inspired, they need to be clear on what you expect from them day-to-day and week-to-week and deeply understand how they can meet or even exceed those expectations. Your people might be thinking: What do I need to do to achieve a goal or objective? When do you expect it to be completed? How will I be assessed against it? Give your people the answers to these questions and provide clarity, or else you risk the move from inspired and productive to unmotivated and underperforming.

Break it up

A tip shared with me by Ben Davies, a U.K. Fitness Consultant, is to break down expectations and goals down into "non-scale victories" (NSV) which are those small but important achievements. For example, if you're training to run a marathon, it would be that first run, the run you do on a rainy day so that you hit your mile goal for the week, and so on. "If you don't acknowledge and celebrate these NSVs you lose motivation, focus, and often, give up on the goal entirely," says Davies. Keep this in mind as a way to set expectations, but also as a way to create ongoing inspiration, as you can appreciate and recognize these NSVs.

Communicate the "why"

Do you remember the Firefighter boss, moving people from fire to fire with no apparent strategy? A big part of this is that they probably weren't actually fires, but rather situations where the "why" was not explained. Skipping the "why" also undermines how you can inspire your people, because they don't understand why things are being done this way. And when this happens, you don't just face the negative consequences as described under the Firefighter boss, but you'll never be able to inspire your people. In the moment they may be inspired, jumping into the "fire," but those flames of inspiration will be extinguished if there's nothing left to hold on to – the "why" of a situation.

So outside of labeling your "why" as your purpose, take it one step further with other details so that your people can really get behind it. For example, if you're asking people to create a new product to align with your mission of being the best global supplier, explain what this means. Is the "why" because your products are successful in one country but aren't working in others, so new ones need to be designed? Or is the "why" that your competitor has just come out with something new that you now need to create to keep pace? Explain the "why" and they will not only be inspired, but have a better chance of achieving your purpose with new ideas.

Believe in your people

Besides believing in your company's mission, purpose, and values, to truly inspire you need to believe in your people. Your people need to feel your trust and your belief in them, or they won't stand by you (or your company) in your time of need. Here are a few tips to enhance your belief in your people:

1. **Get to know them** – First, and it may seem obvious, is to know your people. Know who they are, what they need, and how they are inspired. By learning what your people value and how they work best, you can find individual and unique ways to support, motivate, and inspire them.

2. **Bring out the building blocks** – Next, bring out your building blocks to show them that you believe in them. For example, show them you Trust and Respect them, how your Communication is grounded with honesty and transparency … you get the idea.

3. **Tell them** – And finally, and again another obvious one, is to tell your people that you believe in them and show them appreciation. There's real power to this, as our next study will show.

High expectations (and beliefs) lead to high performance

A study[74] was designed and conducted to find out what would happen to students when their teachers believed that they had high potential. Having tested all the children's cognitive abilities, measuring their verbal and reasoning skills, the researchers selected a sample of children at random, and informed the teachers that these were children of high academic potential, or what they called "intellectual bloomers."

At the end of the school year, all of the students retook the test. The "intellectual bloomers" had improved the most, in fact, some students who were randomly labeled as bloomers achieved more than 50% intelligence gains in a single year. This indicates that the teachers' expectations constituted a contributory variable in the student outcomes and that even inconspicuous factors such as attitude and mood could impact students.

As Adam Grant explains in his book *Give and Take*, "Teachers' beliefs created self-fulfilling prophecies. When teachers believed their students were bloomers, they set high expectations for their success. As a result, the teachers engaged in more supportive behaviors that boosted the students' confidence and enhanced their learning and development."

NEXT STEPS

☐ Assess how well your people understand your company's purpose and direction. Are they clear, or is there more you need to do so that you're all working towards the same north star?

☐ Help each of your people understand how their individual role supports the purpose and goals of the company and in your team. Show them how they're making a difference.

---

74   R. Rosenthal and L. Jacobson, *Pygmalion in the classroom*, 1968.

☐ What can you do going forward to ensure that clear expectations are set and become part of the day-to-day within your team? How can you better adjust them or bring them into outcomes to help your people do their best work?

☐ What can you do to inspire your people as they achieve milestones or face challenges? Can you leverage how you approach other building blocks and tools, such as Appreciation and Communication to guide and motivate them?

WHERE TO BEGIN

Well, we've reached the end of our building blocks. We know that it was a lot to take in, but as we said at the beginning, each of these 14 building blocks can and will help you out of your bad boss traits. So what's next? Where do you start? Here are three steps to help keep you on track as you develop your plan:

1. **Set focus areas** – The first thing to do is to prioritize the building blocks, determining which ones you should focus on based on any bad boss traits you may have, and thus the areas and opportunities for development and improvement. If you completed the online test, this will be done for you automatically (you can find it at www.badbossesruinlives. com). If you have not, in Appendix A we've provided an offline tool you can use.

2. **Reality check** – Next, you'll want to do a reality check of these priorities, taking a step back and making sure that they're the right ones for you. You can do this yourself, but you may also want to run them by your people and your own boss, getting their input and thoughts on whether the priorities have been set correctly, and then adjust accordingly.

3. **Develop a plan** – And finally, you'll want to develop a plan. How will you get to where you need to be? Again, we've developed a tool to help you with this, which you can find in Appendix B.

CONCLUSION

We've come to the end of the book, and let us begin by thanking you. Thank you for being brave enough to pick up a book that so boldly talks about bad bosses, especially with a title saying that they ruin lives. It shows your interest and commitment to this important topic, putting aside any ego and fears that you may have. And thank you for taking time out of your busy schedule to read it. We know that as a boss you have little to no spare time, so this shows how you are already putting your people first.

We hope that at this point, you have lots of phrases highlighted and pages earmarked, ready to refer to if and when you need a bit of inspiration and help. Open it up when things get difficult, when you face a new challenge, or when one of your bad boss traits creeps back in. It's going to happen whether you like it or not, and at times it may not be easy.

But don't give up, remember all of the benefits of being a great boss, and the damages of being a bad boss, and always lean into action. Take one small step, tackle one building block at a time. Do what it takes to be a great boss, one that enriches lives, and not a bad one, who ruins lives. Make that decision every day, what kind of boss do *you* want to be?

WHAT TO DO NEXT

As you finish the book, here is a reminder of what you can do next to continue your journey towards being a great boss:

- **Awareness** – Take the online assessment that can be found at www.badbossesruinlives.com or appearing in Appendix A to understand which bad boss traits you may have.

- **Acceptance** – Review the results of your assessment (either online or in Appendix A) to help you understand which building blocks you should focus on.

- **Action** – Develop your action plan, referring to Appendix B.

ACKNOWLEDGEMENTS

This book has been a true collaborative effort, and for that we are most grateful.

Let us start out by thanking those of you who were kind enough to let us interview you or share content for the book, we really appreciate your insights. Here they are in alphabetical order: Andy Follows, Aoife O'Brien, Ben Whitter, Clare Edwards, Claude Silver, Dana Cavalea, David Berz, Denise Hanlon, Enrique Rubio, Eric Hutcherson, Eric Severson, Garry Ridge, Dr. Grace Lordan, Guy Brazier, Herdis Pala Palsdottir, John Blakey, Kellie Egan, Kim Scott, Kristel Modedt, Marcel Schwantes, Mathew Paine, Nicolas Janni, Sue Kemp, Tracie Sponenberg and Zahed Kamathia.

Let us also thank our editor Chloe Thompson, you were absolutely brilliant at making our words and ideas come to life, so much better than we could have done on our own. And to our talented designer, Colin Goad, Creative Director at MGA Group, who was able to turn concepts that were in our heads into a fantastic cover design, and graphics for the book. What a dream team!

And finally, let us thank the authors of the books that we used for our research. You'll see quotes from them scattered throughout the book, but we thought it would be helpful to have them in one place so that you can use them to continue your learning journey. They are listed below in alphabetical order:

- *Breaking Through: Communicating to Open Minds, Move Hearts, and Change the World* by Sally Susman

- *Build it: The Rebel Playbook for Employee Engagement* by Glenn Elliott and Debra Corey

- *Coaching for Performance* by Sir John Whitmore

- *Compassionate Leadership* by Rasmus Hougaard and Jacqueline Carter

- *Dare to Lead* by Brené Brown

- *Daring Greatly* by Brené Brown

- *Give and Take* by Adam Grant

- *Good Boss, Bad Boss* by Robert I. Sutton

- *Irresistible: The Seven Secrets of the World's Most Enduring, Employee-Focused Organizations* by Josh Bersin

- *Leaders Eat Last* by Simon Sinek

- *Multipliers* by Liz Wiseman

- *No More Sh*t Managers: Seven steps to a coaching culture* by Jo Wright

- *Radical Candor* by Kim Scott

- *Radical Respect* by Kim Scott

- *Team of Teams* by General Stanley McChrystal

- *The Art of Active Listening* by Heather R. Younger

- *The Infinite Game* by Simon Sinek

- *The Speed of Trust* by Stephen M. R. Covey

- *The Trusted Executive: Nine Leadership Habits that Inspire Results, Relationships and Reputation* by John Blakey

- *True North: Emerging Leader Edition* by Bill George and Zach Clayton

- *Turn the Ship Around* by L. David Marquet

- *Unleashed* by Frances Frei and Anne Morriss

Thank you all, your thoughts and inspiration will help make each and every one of us a great boss, ridding the world of bad bosses!

APPENDIX A

BUILDING BLOCK FOCUS AREA EXERCISE

This exercise will help you prioritize the 14 building blocks explained in the book. At the end, you'll have a list of focus blocks to help you improve on any bad boss traits you may have, and be the great boss you want and need to be.

> **Take the assessment online**
>
> Please note that we created a free online assessment that you can use in place of this exercise. You can find it at www.BADBOSSESRUINLIVES.com

Step 1 - Identify your bad boss traits

The first step is to determine which bad boss traits you may have based on the 10 types of bad bosses. You may have done this as you read Part 1, as it was listed as an action at the end, but if you haven't, please keep reading.

Action: For each of the bad boss types, score yourself and write the results in the table below based on the following scoring system:

- **1** – I have **no** traits for this type of bad boss

- **2** – I have **some** traits for this type of bad boss

- **3** – I have **many** of the traits of this type of bad boss

As you do this, it's important to be honest with yourself, remembering that we all have some bad boss traits, so accept them and think of it as an opportunity, and not a punishment. Embrace, and don't ignore these bad boss traits, for that will take you one step closer to being a great boss.

Avoider		Blocker	
Ignorer		Firefighter	
Hoarder		Micromanager	
Unappreciater		Blamer	
Pretender		Coercer	

Step 2 - Understand building block focus areas

The next step is where we share with you the suggested building block focus areas for each of the 10 types of bad bosses. These were determined based on how much of an impact each can have in helping you improve and develop the traits required to eliminate bad boss traits.

Important notes:

- Keep in mind that this does not mean that the other building blocks are not important, it's just that these have more of a direct impact.

- Keep in mind that this is a generic list, so it has not been personalized for you.

Action: Take your scores from Step 1, and add them to the table below.

Type of Bad Boss	Step 1 Score	Top 4 Building Blocks to Focus On			
Avoider		Vulnerability	Communication	Feedback	Development
Ignorer		Empathy	Respect	Listening	Appreciation
Hoarder		Vulnerability	Trust	Communication	Development
Unappreciater		Compassion	Appreciation	Coaching	Inspiration
Pretender		Authenticity	Feedback	Coaching	Empowerment
Blocker		Compassion	Development	Coaching	Inspiration
Firefighter		Empathy	Respect	Empowerment	Inspiration
Micromanager		Trust	Development	Coaching	Empowerment
Blamer		Authenticity	Respect	Communication	Feedback
Coercer		Empathy	Vulnerability	Respect	Listening

Step 3 - Determine preliminary building block focus areas

The next step is to determine the building blocks that you should focus on. You'll do this for your top bad boss types, meaning those that you scored the highest. For some people, this may be those that you scored yourself a 3, and for others, it may be a combination of 3's and 2's.

Action: For each of your top bad boss types, go to the previous table and look through the building blocks that have been listed (e.g. For Avoider, it would be Vulnerability, Communication, Feedback and Development). From these, take the top three to five to use for your preliminary development plan.

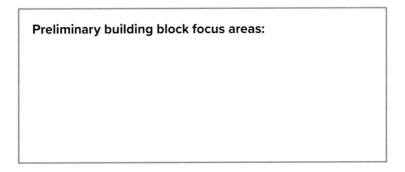

Preliminary building block focus areas:

Step 4 - Determine final building block focus areas

The final step is to do a reality check of these priorities, taking a step back and making sure that they're the right ones for you. You can do this yourself, but you may also want to run them by your people and your boss, getting their input and thoughts on whether the priorities have been set right. Use all of this to adjust and adapt your building block focus areas.

Action: After doing the reality check, list your final building block focus areas in the table below.

> **Final building block focus areas:**

APPENDIX B

GREAT BOSS PROJECT PLAN

This exercise will help you develop your project plan so that you can set and achieve your goals to overcome bad boss traits, and develop more of your great boss ones.

Step 1 - Set your goals

The first step is to set yourself goals for each of your building block focus areas. This step is critical as it will provide clear direction and structure for the rest of your project plan. Where possible, try to work on one or two goals at a time. Changing too many things at once could be confusing, and make it hard to see what changes were most effective.

Actions:

1. Write your building blocks in the first column, transferring them from either your online assessment or from completing Appendix A.

2. For each building block, list the goals you will set to help you improve in this area. As with any goal, make sure each is specific and achievable, and is truly driving the results you are aiming for.

3. For each goal, list what resources you will use, e.g. books, training classes, other people.

4. For each goal, set a timeline to mark when you will achieve it. Make sure they are realistic so that you set yourself up for success.

Building Block	Goal	Resources	Timeline
Example: Appreciation	Meet with my people to understand what appreciation means to them, adding this information to their employee profiles. Schedule time every Friday to send out appreciation notes.	Read a book on appreciation. Attend a company training class on how to write appreciation notes.	By the end of the month Ongoing

Step 2 - Set your metrics

The next step is to set your metrics for each of your goals, deciding what it will look like when you achieve them.

Action: For each goal, list out the metrics, thinking broadly about what you want and need to achieve.

Goal	Metrics
Example: Meet with my people to understand what appreciation means to them.	In the company employee engagement survey, scores increase by at least 5% for the question - I feel my boss appreciates and values me.

Step 3 - Measure progress

After you've achieved some progress, whether it's big or small, it's time to reflect on how far you've come. Recognizing what has gone well, and what are areas for improvement. By doing this, you can then get yourself back on track, adjusting goals, timelines, resources, etc. as necessary.

Actions:

1. For each goal, list the progress you've made against it. Include what you've achieved, to celebrate, and what more work needs to happen.

2. Based on your progress, list what actions you need to take to get to where you want to be. Based on what you write, you may want to go back and adjust your goal, resources, and timelines.

Goal	Progress	Actions to take
Example: Meet with my people to understand what appreciation means to them.	Employee engagement score has gone up by 1% for the question relating to appreciation. This is good, but more work needs to be done to achieve the goal of a 5% increase.	Have another conversation with my people to understand what's working and not working, adapting my approach accordingly.